AFTER THE CEASEFIRES

Brian Lennon SJ

After the Ceasefires

CATHOLICS AND THE FUTURE
OF NORTHERN IRELAND

the columba press

First edition, 1995, published by
the columba press
93 The Rise, Mount Merrion, Blackrock, Co Dublin

Cover by Bill Bolger
Origination by The Columba Press
Printed in Ireland by Colour Books, Dublin

ISBN 1 85607 122 7

Acknowledgements

I would like to thank everyone who helped in different ways in the writing of this book, especially Gerry O'Hanlon, Edel O'Kennedy, Brian Murtagh, Joe McKeever, Martina Killeavy, Tim Hamilton and Cathy Molloy, all of whom read different sections of the text and made helpful comments. Ray Lawler also deserves special thanks for proof-reading.

I am also very grateful to the members of the various groups mentioned in the introduction. Much of the book has arisen as a result of reflections in these groups. This is particularly the case with many of my neighbours in Portadown and with the Drumcree Faith and Justice group.

I would like to thank the members of my Jesuit community, especially Brian MacCuarta who prepared the index, the Presentation sisters in Portadown, Mgr Alex Manly and the people of St Joseph's parish in Long Island, who offered help, encouragement and space for writing.

Contents

Preface

This book looks critically but, I hope, constructively at the Catholic/Nationalist community, especially in Northern Ireland. The same task needs to be done for the British/Protestant/Unionist community. Some of the criticisms that I make of the Nationalist community have at times been made by others who accept in a very uncritical way values of the British state. What I try to do is not only to offer criticisms but to show possible alternatives, which, if adopted, would allow Ireland, North and South, to practise statecraft in a way radically different from that currently practised at Westminster. I see no reason why this should not be possible even if Northern Ireland is to remain part of the UK. But for this to happen, Northern Ireland people, both Nationalist and Unionist, will need to work together.

As regards terminology, the following points should be born in mind: I refer to God using both male and female attributes at different points in the text. I sometimes use 'the North' and 'the South' to refer to Northern Ireland and the Republic. While these terms are not strictly accurate, the use of them makes for easier reading than would be the case by constantly repeating the correct term. Similarly, when I refer to Protestants, I include the Church of Ireland. I hope that this will not cause offence among those members of the church who stress they are as much part of the Catholic Church as the Roman Church is.

Introduction

By 1994, nearly 3500 people had been killed in the Northern Ireland/British-Irish conflict since its latest phase started in 1968. Yet 1994 was also the year of greatest hope for over twenty-five years because in that year both the IRA and loyalist paramilitaries announced a ceasefire. It is difficult to describe how much this meant to a community that had been deeply traumatised.

At the same time important aspects of the causes of the conflict persisted. In deciding to renounce violence, the republican movement did not accept, at least initially, that the constitutional status of Northern Ireland should be decided by the majority of its people. While this principle had been agreed by the Dublin and London governments in the Downing Street Declaration of December 1993, it had not been enshrined in the Irish Constitution. Further, the depth of bitterness between the two communities remained.

This book asks what tasks Catholics face in responding to the political and social realities of Northern Ireland and its relationship with both Britain and the south. To do this we need to approach the issue from two different perspectives: the theological and the political. The book is therefore interdisciplinary. The basic thesis is that reconciliation and justice – to be real – must go together. It is impossible to have true reconciliation without justice, or true justice without reconciliation. My contention is that this can be illustrated politically in the Northern Ireland conflict and it can also be shown to be true in Christian theology. Bringing insights from each discipline to bear on the other should help our reflections in both areas.

The particular theological themes that I have selected are some of the great themes of the scriptures and of Christian tradition: the fact that God is a community of three persons, the liberation that God wants to bring to all, especially to the most deprived, the inclusiveness of God, the call of God to all of us to forgive our enemies, the conflict, suffering and failure that all this entails, and the ultimate triumph of God's love. I will argue that these themes in practice do not dominate our lives and our church as Catholics sufficiently.

9

In our context in Ireland, there is a major need for reconciliation. That much is obvious. But what does that mean? What does it mean in the area of politics? What is the task of the church and of Catholics as individuals in this area? In what way should our scriptural insights influence our politics?

To answer these questions I look at some of the main dilemmas facing Irish nationalists after the 1994 ceasefires. These are issues about which there is as yet insufficient agreement on this island. These are: the area of the nation state, the issue of consent, political structures within Northern Ireland and between the north and the south, policing in Northern Ireland, and the question of minorities.

All of these were unresolved issues at the time of the ceasefires. Can the scriptures help us to deal with them? What sort of faith should we bring to bear on them? What sort of faith do we currently bring to bear on them? What images of God are in our minds as we approach them?

Background experiences

My interest in Northern Ireland developed during a year I spent in the US in the mid-1970s. Born and bred a Dubliner, my knowledge and experience of the situation was remote, despite having a grand-father who was born in Saul, near Downpatrick, and who spent his working life in the north. My experience in the US was one of looking at my country from afar and meeting Irish Americans who had simplistic notions of the 'Green Isle' and 'Brits out'. This experience changed me. I felt if I was to work for gospel values anywhere in the world it should be in Northern Ireland, given the level of suffering and division that existed there.

As it happened, the Jesuit Order had been trying for some years to open a house in the north. There were various ecclesiastical diffi-culties with this, but in 1980 Cardinal Ó Fiaich warmly invited us to Portadown. This was just over a year after my ordination and coin-cided with the completion of my studies at the Irish School of Ecumenics in Dublin. With two others, I was asked to form the new community.

Six months after our arrival we moved into Churchill Park. This was a deprived area of the town and almost completely Catholic. In deciding where to live, we had two principles: one was that we should be living among the most deprived people in the town. A second was that our work should be ecumenical. By living in Churchill Park we learnt how rich people's lives can be even though they live in very difficult circumstances. We made close friendships, and we learnt something about how to be priests, mainly by learning more about our own humanity. We also learnt about conflict and fear, and we had a lot of fun as well.

Churchill Park, it turned out, was not at all as rough as its detractors had alleged. By standards of cities such as Dublin, Belfast or Manchester, for example, its social problems were minor, mainly because of its size – a small housing estate of about 250 houses. But it had problems. The number of sectarian murders was less in the 1980s than in the 1970s, but there were still plenty of riots. One of our early tasks was to attempt mediation in the middle of these, often late at night.

In the summer of 1981, during a bonfire to commemorate the anniversary of internment, the RUC fired nearly 135 plastic bullets at a group made up mainly of women and youths. They alleged afterwards that their lives were endangered by the crowd. This was certainly not true because I was standing among the police. I had moved there to try to persuade them to stop firing, and had their lives been in danger I regret to say I would not have stayed! We followed up this particular incident with a well-documented complaint which got nowhere. It was our first introduction to the inadequacies of the policing system and also to the depth of feeling against the police. At the same time we learnt something of the problems the RUC had in policing a divided society.

Naturally, contact with our neighbours was a key element in forming our picture of the situation. They had strong views on the whole Northern Ireland conflict. An important local issue in the mid-1980s was Orange marches. These were routed through nationalist areas by the RUC and British army and were deeply resented by locals. In response a small number of people formed the Drumcree Faith and Justice Group. The dialogues within this group had an immense influence on my own learning and thinking about the conflict. As a group they were willing to confront justice issues, especially where they felt they affected young people. At the same time they sought out and entered into dialogue with Protestant/ unionists in order to learn about their perspective. Prayer was important in the group, because there were many times when feelings were intense and this made it extremely difficult to listen to some of the demands of the gospel about peace, forgiveness, reconciliation and justice.

With an unemployment rate of 90% within the local housing estate, and of over 70% in the surrounding area, many of the problems were connected with poverty. Within the Catholic community people tended to look down on Churchill Park, and in turn its residents often internalised these views. This sense of inferiority was so strong in the early 1980s that some of the residents would get off the bus a stop early, because they were ashamed to say that they were living in Churchill Park.

A second element in our experience was the Protestant community. At first we made contact with them through the clergy fraternal which continued to meet throughout the riots that took place over Orange marches. This was a group composed of most, though not all, the clergy in the town. Some of the clergy, who were opposed to ecumenical contacts, met in a separate fraternal. It was a good experience of learning to respect and to pray with people with whom I often disagreed deeply. Contacts in the clergy fraternal also led to the development of several initiatives within Portadown: a series of dialogues with members of different churches; Project Portadown, a cross-community group whose aim is to develop on-going contacts; and the involvement of representatives of the Protestant community in economic development with Drumcree Co-operative: this was a group set up within the nationalist area to develop youth and adult education, community development and economic initiatives.

In the early years we experienced much confusion. This is inevitable in a situation of conflict. The need for groups to reflect on the political aspects of the conflict from a theological perspective seemed obvious. In time this need led a small number of us – Catholics and Protestants, nationalists and unionists, from both north and south – to form the Interchurch Group on Faith and Politics in 1983. It became an important space for me to explore my own faith and political ideas, and the interaction between them. It was also a group in which we learned to make space for each other. By 1993 the group had published seven different agreed documents.[1]

The Faith and Politics group helped dialogue in our local area. Some time after the publication of *Breaking Down the Enmity*, the group's first document, I went through it with the Drumcree Group and asked them to respond to it. Over the course of a year they did this and published the result in *The story of a journey*.[2] This was critical of a middle class bias in the Faith and Politics Group's document, but also accepted the validity of many of the issues raised by *Enmity*. The document ended up with a discussion of policing. While it refused to accept the RUC, it saw that nationalists had a responsibility to take part in policing and this left the group with a

dilemma which they could not answer. This, for me, was a powerful example of people tackling a problem with honesty, and being
willing to admit that they did not have all the answers.

A further element in our learning was the prisoners in the Maze
prison (Long Kesh). We used to say Mass on Sundays in the prison,
when needed. This was often a tense experience, especially during
the time of the 1981 hunger strike which reached its peak shortly
after we arrived in Northern Ireland. Very often we would have
long conversations with prisoners before or after Mass. There was
deep and vehement disagreement between the IRA and clergy, a
disagreement that persisted until the IRA declared a ceasefire.
Prisoners felt that they were being spoken down to, that clergy and
the hierarchy were backing the British government and were selec-
tive in their condemnation of violence, and that they were biassed
towards the middle-classes. The clergy, for their part, believed that
the IRA campaign was immoral and had to be condemned. It was
more important to the Catholic clergy to condemn violence from
their own side than from that of the unionist community, which
they felt was the task – often neglected – of the Protestant community.
At the same time I felt that it was important to challenge abuses by
the security forces.

In this context, talking at Mass in the prison or in the parish,
about peace, justice, reconciliation, forgiveness, and conflict, was
painful and difficult. Nonetheless these were the themes that began
to emerge in my own mind early on in my journey in the north and
this book is an attempt to reflect critically on them in the light of our
experience.

Two other groups have deeply influenced the reflections in this
book. One was a small group of working-class Protestants. They
showed me something of the depth of anger that exists within the
Protestant community and also that the suffering in deprived working-class Protestant areas is very similar to that of Catholic areas.

Another group which influenced me is the Signs of the Times
Group. Originally made up only of Jesuits, it expanded to include,
and eventually to have a majority of, lay people. Its aim was to
reflect on social, economic, educational and political issues in the
light of theology. One part of this reflection led to my writing, with
three other Jesuits, *Solidarity, the missing link in Irish society*.[3] This
was an effort to look at some economic and political themes in the
island as a whole. A second thrust in this group has been the reflections of women, influenced by feminism, from both better-off and
more deprived backgrounds. Given the social divisions both north

and south, it is striking the degree to which women from different backgrounds can enter into an almost intuitive communication about ways in which they have experienced discrimination. Their insights have been important in opening up new aspects of God to me, and in emphasising the fact that, if we are to make any progress within the north, it can only be on the basis of new and more inclusive, just relationships.

Finally, in 1991 I became involved with the Religious for Justice and Peace group. This was a number of religious from Larne, Belfast, Portadown and Newry. Many of them were living and working in deprived areas. Several of them had worked in Latin America. There was a common vision among the group about the importance of deprived people in God's community, the need to work for justice, and the necessity of building relationships in which both Protestants and Catholics felt at home. It was an important group to me as a support and I also saw it as potentially very important in raising questions for the church in Northern Ireland.

The process

This book, then, has arisen from my experience of living in Northern Ireland for fourteen years. That experience raised political and social dilemmas. As Christians, it is appropriate that we reflect on these in the light of the Christian story as revealed in the scriptures and the tradition of our community. However, I did not approach the scriptures with a *tabula rasa* or blank slate. I brought to it attitudes and theological beliefs that had developed over years. In turn, the reflection on experience and the scriptures challenged these beliefs.

Structure of the book

There are four sections to the book. In section one I show briefly why reconciliation and justice cannot exist properly without each other: there cannot be full reconciliation without justice, or full justice without reconciliation. This is true politically, because each group sees itself, with some justification, as a minority. I illustrate this by giving a brief overview of the historical background. I then look at the major issues facing Irish nationalists at the time of the 1994 ceasefires: theories of the nation state, the issue of consent, political structures, and minorities.

The next section looks at the themes of reconciliation and justice in the scriptures and in theology, in order to show how these are of central importance to the Christian God. I have divided this into seven sections:

1. God as a community of three persons who want us to become part of their community;
2. God as a liberator who brings justice to the community;
3. God as inclusive of all peoples;
4. God as the reconciler who cannot bear hatred and division between his children;
5. The God of conflict;
6. The God who suffers and fails, and
7. The God who triumphs.

In each of these, I outline in part what the scriptures say. I argue that what we see in the scriptures is a God of community who is infinitely concerned about the type of communities that we create. Ultimately, I suggest that God is so caught up in the need for reconciliation that he is incapable of letting any of us go, so that if necessary he will wait for all eternity for us to repent, to turn towards him and to enter into communion with all his children.

But this must not blind us to God's concern for justice. God's anger is vehement against those who oppress others. This is a constant theme of both the Hebrew scriptures and of the gospels. Yet this anger is within the context of God's continued love, even for those who commit oppression.

In the final two sections I attempt to integrate the scriptural and political vision that has emerged. I apply the conclusions first to the vocation of Irish nationalists who are members of the Catholic Church. I suggest changes in the area of church and worship, and secondly in the relationship between church and society. I believe changes are necessary for the church to become more like God's community on earth. For this to happen there is need for a deep commitment to both reconciliation and justice. This means changing relations within the church, for example with deprived groups and women. It means being open to greater pluralism of ideas and debate. It means changing our understanding of the eucharist. It means placing a much greater emphasis on ecumenical work as central to the life of the church. In short, it means changing our understanding of community. I argue that changing our relationships within the institutional church, and our priorities, could make a major impact on reconciliation and justice in society at large.

Secondly, I suggest ways in which Catholics as members of society might respond to the constitutional and political issues that confront us. I suggest that if we take both our scriptural and our political analysis seriously, we will exclude Irish-only or British-only solutions because they take seriously neither the need for reconciliation nor for justice. Nor do they face the fact that each of the minorities in the conflict – northern nationalists and unionists – have an effect-ive veto on such proposals. I examine some positive suggestions that attempt to take account of the needs and identities of each com-munity and ask how they would work in practice. Clearly others, with equal commitment to reconciliation and justice, could come up with different proposals.

The discussion will concentrate on the Catholic Church and nationalists, because that is the community to which I belong. I will be asking what we in the Irish, Catholic – and mostly nationalist – community can do to become more free, to live more justly, to build better relationships with other groups. Other churches and groups need to ask similar questions, and in a more searching way than they have done to date. Just as this book attempts to raise questions for the Catholic community out of the context of our faith, so there is a continuing need for a similar exercise within Protestant Churches.

Notes:
1. These were published as a collection in *Breaking Down the Enmity,* Belfast: Interchurch Group on Faith and Politics, 7 Upper Crescent, 1993.
2. Portadown: Drumcree Faith and Justice Group, 211 Churchill Park, 1991.
3. Dublin: Jesuit Centre for Faith and Justice, 1993.

SECTION I:
The problem

CHAPTER 1

Why reconciliation and justice must go together

A double minority

If we are to make a positive impact on the northern conflict I believe we need to keep in mind *both* reconciliation *and* justice. In practice they are often separated, so that people argue for justice without any attempt to work for reconciliation, or else speak of the need for reconciliation without challenging the changes that are required in our relationships before reconciliation can take place.

Theologically, the reason why reconciliation and justice must go together is that they are two sides of the same coin: the God who longs to be reconciled with us is the same God whose anger is provoked at our oppression of each other.

Politically, it is also true that reconciliation and justice must go together. Among Irish nationalists the demand for justice is a central theme. This is because they have suffered much both in the past from British imperialism and also from the continued injustice of many present-day British government decisions. The demand for justice is then a rallying cry to bring together those who oppose injustice.

However, the reality is that in the Northern Ireland conflict there are two minorities, each of which suffers injustice, and not one.

Nationalists are a minority within Northern Ireland. From the middle of the nineteenth century, the industrialisation of Belfast attracted large numbers of poor Catholics into the city. While at first there was a degree of harmony between Protestants and Catholics, economic rivalry and sectarianism gradually came to the fore. This was strengthened by the political fears of Protestants during the Home Rule debates of 1886 and 1893. In the south, the movement for national independence did not really gather strength until 1912, although Arthur Griffith founded Sinn Féin in 1906. Pearse's blood sacrifice in the 1916 rebellion, which was designed to restore the belief of Irishmen in their nation, achieved its result. But what was increasingly obvious in the period up to 1921 was that independence mattered more to nationalists than unity.

18

Because of this, the most important conflict was between northern unionists and *southern* nationalists. Two other groups were forgotten in this conflict: southern unionists and northern nationalists. While the former were able to solve their situation by either leaving the Free State or accepting it, the latter – much greater in number – made no such choice. They stayed. But they did not accept the northern state. Nor did the northern state accept them.

From 1921 to 1969, the northern minority looked to the south to complete the task the southern state claimed to have set itself: gaining the independence of the whole country. But the south had its own problems. It had been riven by the Civil War between 1921 and 1923. While this ended with the defeat of the republicans and the subsequent entry of De Valera into the Dáil in 1926 and into power in 1932, the divisions of the Civil War remained the dominant feature of southern politics, at least until Sean Lemass became Taoiseach. The south was therefore much more concerned with its own internal affairs than it was with Northern Ireland. The separate experiences of each part of the country during World War II added to the psychological distance between them.

The period up to the 1960s saw the southern state established on a firm footing. The contradictions in southern policy during this period have been outlined by Clare O'Halloran.[1] No attempt was made by the southern government from 1927 on to make serious contact with northern politicians. While an effort had been made in the early days of 1922 by Michael Collins to accept the implications of unity by having the southern government pay the salaries of northern nationalist teachers who opted out of the northern educational system, this was dropped after a few months. Thereafter it was tacitly accepted that while the southern government would continue to look for world pressure to be brought on the British government to end partition, it would not interfere in Northern Ireland affairs. This was not because the south accepted the northern state, but simply because nothing else was possible. In these circumstances, it was something of an embarrassment when northern nationalists appeared in Dublin and the government frequently refused to see them.

Sean Lemass's decision in 1965 to travel north to see northern Premier Terence O'Neill was taken as an Irish nationalist. But his action was against the tradition of his ideology and in that sense was designed to change the tradition. But he could not have foreseen the difficulty involved in taking an ideology that had served its purpose in winning independence for the south of the country

and changing it to take due account, not only of northern nationalists, but also of northern unionists. Those difficulties became more
obvious in 1969, when his successor Jack Lynch said the south
would 'not stand idly by' as northern security forces attacked
Catholics in Derry, and then showed himself powerless to prevent
such attacks.

Northern nationalists therefore saw themselves as having been
cut off from their fellow country men and women in 1920. They had
been excluded from exercising political power within Northern
Ireland for all but four months of its 75 years of existence.

But Protestants are also a minority. The history of the last 300
years on this island is one that saw Protestants in the ascendant
from the victory of William of Orange over King James at the Battle
of the Boyne in 1690 until the passing of the Catholic Emancipation
Act in 1829, which gave the vote to Catholics. Protestants remained
in power in practice up to 1921 in the south and up to 1972 in the
north, but the decline of their power was inevitable from 1829 on.
What the last 200 years has shown is the retreat of Protestants to the
north-east corner of the island. Even within Northern Ireland they
have moved from the west and from border counties – often in
response to IRA attacks – to areas east of Belfast. Next to that is the
Irish Sea. Psychologically, the Protestant community has for many
years feared annihilation or expulsion from the island.

While Protestants make up about 58% of the population within
Northern Ireland, they are only 25% of the population of the island
as a whole. They have felt threatened, understandably, by the IRA.
They fear the south's ambitions in relation to the north. They fear
the Catholic Church, and see it, somewhat incredibly to the insider,
as a strong, monolithic institution dedicated to the overthrow of
Protestantism. Their experience on the island for the past 200 years
has been one of a loss of power and influence, both institutionally
and geographically.

Within the north from 1921-1969, fear of the south among
Protestants, fuelled in part by the south's statements on the north,
remained dominant. This was allied to a fear of Catholics and the
possible re-emergence of the IRA as a potent force.

The situation is complicated by relationships between the
Dublin and London governments and the limited clarity about the
status of Northern Ireland. This required two separate versions of
the Anglo-Irish Agreement to be signed in 1985, because the two
sides did not agree on whether Northern Ireland should be
described as part of the United Kingdom or not. The relationships

between each government and its respective client within the north are also ambivalent.

In this context it becomes increasingly difficult to see how there can be any justice until there is reconciliation. Without political reconciliation, 'justice' becomes something which one disaffected group tries to take from the other.

The Civil Rights Movement

The present phase of the British-Irish conflict – euphemistically referred to as 'The Troubles' – began in 1969. While we are still far too close to these events to write proper history about them, nonetheless it is clear that a number of factors coalesced. One was the emergence of the Civil Rights movement in the USA. A second was the relatively new existence of television media. A third was a new-found confidence among Catholics, a confidence which was crucially influenced by the Education Act of 1948 which made it possible for the first time for many Catholics to avail of third level education. Fourthly, Protestant fundamentalism, the deep insecurity of the northern state, British colonial attitudes, and the traditional nationalist interpretation of the conflict, all conspired to ensure that the conflict, while it might for a while take on the appearance of a civil rights struggle, would soon be dominated once again by constitutional issues.

The context of the Civil Rights movement in the US was fundamentally different from the British-Irish conflict, precisely because the US struggle was about the Constitution. The vision that Martin Luther King had was of the possibilities that the existing US Constitution gave of freedom for his people. Freedom meant, not a state independent of the US, but the winning of rights due to black people, as American citizens. The struggle of American blacks obviously appealed to oppressed groups throughout the world, including northern Irish nationalists. Given their new found education and the sense of optimism in the late 1960s, it is not surprising that nationalists decided that their situation under the Stormont government was intolerable, and, further, that they could resolve their problems through peaceful demonstrations.

Constitutional issues were left to one side. The aim was to allow Irish nationalists the same rights as other British citizens. Whether or not Irish nationalists would accept this was a secondary question. But this was not the way that the Protestant unionist community and its government responded. Initially some Protestants joined the civil rights movement. Because of the insecurity they felt as a

minority within the context of the whole island, the majority of
Protestants saw the civil rights movement as simply the old nationalist struggle under a new guise. They reacted, therefore, in their
traditional manner of oppression. Catholics were burnt out of their
homes in Belfast. The civil rights march to Burntollet, in January
1969, was attacked by stone-throwing and baton-wielding mobs,
some of whom were members of the security forces. The Battle of
the Bogside showed an armed police force attacking an unarmed
civilian population, whose only response were barricades, stones,
and petrol bombs. Worldwide sympathy, including British senti-
ment, was clearly on the side of the nationalists in the early part of
the struggle.

It is not clear exactly when and how the IRA became involved.
However it would be wrong to think of the IRA as an outside force
waiting for the opportune moment to come in and take over the
movement. Members of the IRA were part of the local communities
in Derry and Belfast. Their thinking and activity was part of the
civil rights movement from the beginning. This does not mean that
they were active in the IRA at that stage, or that they saw armed
struggle as inevitable. Like everyone else, their thinking evolved in
a fast-changing situation. What was obvious, however, was that the
nationalist community had no effective protection against armed
unionists, including the security forces. Graffiti on the walls of
Belfast that 'The IRA ran away' were the reaction of people frustrated
and angry at being burnt out of their homes. For many people in
traditionally republican homes, whose families had a frequent history of arrest and internment, the solution was obvious: turn to violence.

The spirituality of non-violence

Those who opposed violence had their case made more difficult by
the violent reaction of the security forces. But the strength of their
argument was much weaker than that of their counterparts in the
US for one other crucial reason. In the US the civil rights movement
was deeply influenced by a pacifist religion. Many of the leaders
were clergy in black churches. King's writings show the extent to
which his commitment to non-violence went far beyond the question of its effectiveness. In Northern Ireland there was no spiritual
movement of similar strength to support non-violence, or if there
was it was certainly not articulated. Robert Coles has told the story
of six-year-old Ruby Bridges in New Orleans in 1960. Ruby was the
only black child sent to a white school. For weeks she was escorted

by federal marshals past angry white mobs and sat in a classroom all day with her one teacher. Her teacher reported to Coles that Ruby's lips were moving as she passed the white hecklers on the sidewalk. Pressed to tell her what she was saying, Ruby replied:

'I was praying for them.'

'Ruby, you pray for the people there?'

'Oh yes.'

'...Why do you do that?'

'Because they need praying for.'

'Why you especially?'

'Because if you're going through what they're doing to you, you're the one who should be praying for them'. And then she quoted to me what she had heard in church. The minister said that Jesus went through a lot of trouble, and he said about the people who were causing the trouble, 'Forgive them, because they don't know what they're doing.' And now little Ruby was saying this in the 1960s, about the people in the streets of New Orleans. How is someone like me supposed to account for that, psychologically, or any other way?'[2]

To what extent were the spiritual resources which the story of Ruby Bridges reveals available to people in the Catholic community in Northern Ireland in 1969? How much was forgiveness a central demand of the type of faith that was practised in the Catholic Church at the time? How much effort was made to understand the needs and fears of the enemy? How much concern was there for justice for Catholics as something that they should work for out of a religious motivation of respect for the rights of all? How many efforts were made to make people aware of the ambiguity of all ideologies, including that of the civil rights movement itself? These are questions that can be asked in retrospect. They would have been very difficult questions to focus on at the time.

In Protestant churches, the silence that had gone on for years about injustices committed against Catholics, and the failure to critique the state, came home to roost at the time of the civil rights movement. In churches within both communities, the community was defined as their own exclusive group. This was not the type of community that Christ had in mind in the gospels.

The movement from a kind of peace to widespread destructive violence was shocking in its speed. In 1969 there were eight explosions, no shootings, and thirteen deaths. Three years later there were 1495 explosions, 10,628 shootings, and 467 deaths.[3] This movement is parallel to the destructiveness of the civil war in former Yugoslavia in 1990-92, when Muslims and Christians, who had formerly lived in relative peace in the same villages, performed appalling deeds on each other within months of the outbreak of war. It suggests both that all humans are capable of such barbaric acts, and that apparently stable political structures can hide deep fissures which may lead unexpectedly to violence unless they are dealt with.

The most serious attempt at political reconciliation between nationalists and unionists between 1968 and 1985 was the Sunningdale Agreement of 1973. This led to the setting up of a power-sharing executive with a Council of Ireland. The three crucial issues in these, as in all subsequent negotiations, were the degree to which nationalists enjoyed power within Northern Ireland, the control of the security forces, and the clarity, or lack of it, of the constitutional relationship with the south.

The degree of nationalist participation in power was high: four out of eleven cabinet seats. (Six went to the unionists and one to the Alliance Party). The control of the security forces remained in the hands of the British government. Internment remained on the statute books. It was unclear what the implications of the Council of Ireland were. The Fine Gael/Labour coalition that was elected in the south in 1973, under the leadership of Liam Cosgrave, emphasised reform rather than the issue of partition in their northern policy. In this they were not radically different from the previous Fianna Fáil administration, led by Jack Lynch, which had emphasised power-sharing in its election manifesto. The SDLP were seriously worried about the southern government's position, which they felt lent support to the minimalist approach of the British government in their White Paper. This saw the Council as a body which would have a role in the co-ordination of 'matters of substantial mutual interest'. But it was made clear that this referred to areas such as tourism, regional development and transport, and also that the Council could only be developed with the assent of the majority within Northern Ireland. By the end of the summer, the SDLP had convinced the southern government to back their demand for substantial powers for the Council, and also their view that the Sunningdale Agreement should be a stage on the path to eventual unity.

However, at the end of the negotiations with the British, the position of the Council had been only marginally strengthened. Nor was there any agreement as to its exact powers and role.

In these circumstances, it is not surprising that the initiative failed in the face of the Ulster Workers' Council strike of 1974. The strike was helped by the fear of a united Ireland and by the opposition of many unionists to power-sharing. The failure of the British army to confront the strikers surprised many at the time and this was another element in the strike's success. This was in marked contrast to the situation in 1977 when Ian Paisley led a second Protestant workers' strike. It failed partly because, under Secretary of State Roy Mason, the army intervened with determination.

Conclusion

This overview shows several themes. One is the grounds each community within Northern Ireland has for seeing itself as a minority.

Just as unionist power has declined since 1969, so nationalists within Northern Ireland have made some political gains. A major reason for this has been the educational achievements of Catholics as a result of the 1948 Education Act, which gave free education up to university level to both Catholics and Protestants. These gains were quite limited politically up to the 1994 ceasefire. In a negative sense, they have taken away unionist domination through Stormont, and replaced it with direct rule from Westminster. But neither nationalists nor unionists have since been able to exercise any direct political power because they have not been able to meet the condition which successive British governments have quite properly laid down for any new devolved government: that both communities would participate in it. However, instruments like the Anglo-Irish Agreement and the Fair Employment Act have made a difference to nationalists both psychologically and, to a limited degree, in practice.

Despite the gains they have made, northern nationalists still see themselves as an abandoned minority. Before 1972 they were excluded from many of the benefits of the state. They suffered discrimination of varying degrees in housing, jobs and the gerrymandering of electoral areas.[4] They still suffer discrimination within the north in jobs and also in the way that their own symbols are given less respect than those of unionists.

The nationalist dream of unity depended on the intervention of the south. That did not happen. The problems of the north were not those of the south, and if verbal republicanism stated that the first national priority of the south was the unity of the country, practical realities dictated otherwise. This happened in part because there was no apparent means to bring about unity except through war.

But in practice precious little effort was made to persuade unionists of the value of unity by non-violent means.

The ambivalent relationship of the southern state towards its northern client-group was matched by a similar ambivalence of the British government towards unionists. The relationship between the two governments was also unclear at different periods, especially since 1969. This in turn increased the insecurity of the two northern groups.

Each community within Northern Ireland, then, sees itself with some justification as a minority and acts with many of the fears and resentments of minority groups in conflict situations throughout the world. Further, the ambivalence of the two governments to their client-groups within Northern Ireland, and towards each other, has contributed to the insecurity of the situation. One of the most promising developments that we shall see in later chapters is a gradual clarification of this relationship between the two governments.

Finally, it is worth noting at this stage that there was little in the type of faith that Catholics practised that could help them to develop a more appropriate political stance. What their faith did was to console them as victims – which was important; it gave them a sense of unity and of perseverance; and it may have helped many of them to renounce violence. But it did not help them to forgive their enemies in advance of any repentance. It did not help them to bring their faith to bear on politics. And it did not help them to link justice with reconciliation. Similar criticisms could also be made of Protestants.

Notes:
1. Clare O'Halloran, *Partition and the limits of Irish nationalism: an ideology under stress*, Dublin: Gill and Macmillan, 1987.
2. Robert Coles, 'The inexplicable prayers of Ruby Bridges', in *Christianity Today*, Vol 29, No 11 (August 1985), pp 19-20, quoted by Donald W. Shriver, Jnr, 'A struggle for justice and reconciliation: forgiveness in the politics of the American Black Civil Rights movement 1955-68', *Studies*, Summer 1989, pp 136-150.
3. Kevin Boyle, Tom Hadden, and Paddy Hillyard, *Ten Years On in Northern Ireland: the legal control of violence*, London: Cobden Trust, 1980, p 15.
4. For a good discussion of the extent of discrimination, and of its limits, *cf* John Whyte, 'How much discrimination was there under the unionist regime, 1921-1968?' in Tom Gallagher and James O'Connell (eds), *Contemporary Irish Studies*, Manchester University Press, 1983.

CHAPTER 2

The major concerns of Irish Nationalism at the 1994 ceasefire

Introduction
In this chapter I want to outline the major concerns that faced Irish nationalists when the IRA ceasefire commenced on 1 September 1994. In it I will look at the nation state and the issue of consent. This second section will look at the movement that took place in relation to consent in the 1983-84 New Ireland Forum, the Anglo-Irish Agreement and the Downing Street Declaration. I will then discuss some of the issues raised by Articles Two and Three of the Republic's Constitution, nationalist and unionist vetoes and the role of the British government.

I will then outline the views of the parties on political structures, especially the principles that should govern them, the issue of security, and the European context.

In the final section I will discuss minorities under two headings: pluralism and the economically deprived.

The nation state
Nationalism is based on the thesis that a people can constitute a nation and, if they do so, they are entitled to form themselves into a state whose territory will be the same as that occupied by the people. Twentieth-century nationalists are following the example of previous centuries when states like Britain, France and the US emerged based broadly on the same principle. The argument put for a united Ireland is similar to that of nationalist movements throughout the world: Ireland is a nation; the area of the nation corresponds with the whole island; it therefore has the right to independent statehood and this right is being frustrated by successive British governments.

However, Sinn Féin and the SDLP differ in their understanding of nationalism. Sinn Féin argues that the 1918 election, in which the Irish people freely chose an independent republic, was the 'last occasion when the Irish people nationally exercised their franchise'[1] and they won the election with 69.5% of the vote. They

argue that the Treaty of 1921, which gave independence to the Free
State and allowed Northern Ireland the right to remain part of the
UK, was forced on an unwilling Irish people by the force of British
arms. It was not submitted to the Irish people for ratification and the
imposition represents a denial to the Irish people of the freedom to
exercise their right of self-determination. Therefore it remains illegit-
imate. Any expression of opinion that has happened since has not
changed this. The Irish people have consistently shown their desire
for unity. Seán McBride, former Chief of Staff of the IRA, believed
that 'Ireland's right to sovereignty, independence and unity are
inalienable and indefeasible. It is for the Irish people as a whole to
determine the future status of Ireland. Neither Britain nor a small
minority selected by Britain has any right to partition the ancient
island of Ireland, nor to determine its future as a sovereign nation'.[2]

Accepting that those living on the island of Ireland constitute a
people, Sinn Féin argues that support for the right of self-determination is to be found in the two UN Covenants of 1966 – on Civil
and Political Rights, and on Economic, Social and Cultural Rights.

For their part, the SDLP see the British government as more neutral than Sinn Féin do. Because of this they have accepted the principle that there shall be no change in the constitutional position of
Northern Ireland without the consent of the majority.

The issue of consent
Republicans argued up to 1994 not only that unionists had no right
to block a United Ireland, but that the only way to persuade them to
accept it was through violence. Once the ceasefire in 1994 was
announced, that option was closed off. But Sinn Féin still refused to
accept the principle that the majority of the people in Northern
Ireland should be entitled to decide its constitutional status.

Unionists argued that unity by consent logically meant that
unionists could refuse it if they chose to do so. 'If we have the right
to say 'yes' to a United Ireland, surely we have the right to say 'no'
to a United Ireland'.[3]

THE NEW IRELAND FORUM

The story of Irish nationalism from 1974 to 1994 is of a gradual,
although incomplete, move towards accepting the principle that
there would be no unity on the island without the consent of the
unionists. The New Ireland Forum Report accepted that the aim of
a united Ireland should only be pursued peacefully and on the basis
of agreement. 'The aim of nationalists, therefore, in seeking Irish

unity is to develop and promote an Irishness that demonstrates convincingly to unionists that the concerns of the unionist and Protestant heritage can be accommodated in a credible way and that institutions can be created which would protect such concerns and provide fully for their legitimate self-expression' (4.6).

The Report recognised that any unity to be achieved 'would require a general and explicit acknowledgement of a broader and more comprehensive Irish identity. Such unity would, of course, be different from both the existing Irish state and the existing arrangement in Northern Ireland because it would necessarily accommodate all the fundamental elements in both traditions.' (5.4).

'The particular structure of political unity which the Forum would wish to see established is a unitary state, achieved by agreement and consent, embracing the whole island of Ireland and providing irrevocable guarantees for the protection and preservation of both the unionist and nationalist identities.' (5.7) The Report recognised that unionists would have to negotiate their role in any arrangements which would embody Irish unity (5.8). The Report also mentioned two other options, a federal/confederal state and joint authority(5.9).

THE ANGLO-IRISH AGREEMENT

The Anglo-Irish Agreement at first sight seemed to go further in accepting that unionist agreement was a pre-condition for unity.

In Article One the two governments:

a) affirm that any change in the status of Northern Ireland would only come about with the consent of a majority of the people of Northern Ireland;

b) recognise that the present wish of a majority of the people of Northern Ireland is for no change in the status of Northern Ireland;

c) declare that, if in the future a majority of the people of Northern Ireland clearly wish for and formally consent to the establishment of a united Ireland, they will introduce and support in the respective Parliaments legislation to give effect to that wish.

At first sight this Article seems to give unionists all they are looking for: Northern Ireland is currently part of the UK; there will be no change in this as long as the majority want it to remain as such; and unionists are in the majority. However, unionists make the point that there is no agreement among the signatories to the Agreement as to what the status of Northern Ireland is: the

Republic sees it as part of the Irish national territory, and under Article Three of the south's Constitution it is, in their view, merely waiting for the re-unification of the country for the laws of the Dáil to be applied to Northern Ireland.

Secondly, the UK government has made different stipulations in regard to the other countries that make up the UK: in the case of the referendum in both Scotland and Wales in 1979 a devolved parliament would have been set up if 40% of the population, together with a majority of those who actually voted, had approved it. This is quite different from the simple majority required in Northern Ireland, although it is not clear whether it is a majority of the population or of voters that is required. Unlike Scotland and Wales, the Agreement offers the Northern Ireland electorate only one choice if they decide to leave the UK: becoming part of a united Ireland. In these circumstances their uncertainty about the long-term intentions of the British government is increased.

From the point of view of the Irish government, Article One meant that they did not have to redefine Articles Two and Three of the Republic's Constitution. The Irish were conscious of the Sunningdale Agreement, the constitutionality of which had been tested in the Irish Supreme Court by Kevin Boland.

Article One of the Agreement is in effect a fudge. It is at the centre of the British-Irish conflict. Removing the uncertainty contained in it is essential for there to be peace. There are some who argue against this on the grounds that uncertainty, and some fudging, is necessary in international relations, especially when dealing with issues as emotive as nationalism. They have a point in that there is a fundamentalist desire for certainty that can never, and never should, be satisfied. However, the degree of uncertainty, given the history of the relationship between the two countries, and the violence of northern paramilitaries, is too great for there to be much chance of progress without reducing this uncertainty.

THE DOWNING STREET DECLARATION

The issue of consent emerged again with the Downing Street Declaration, signed in December 1993. The Declaration was a carefully crafted document. It differed from the Anglo-Irish Agreement in several ways. Firstly it was not an international treaty and so had much less status. Secondly, it did not set up new structures of government. Thirdly, unionists were consulted about its contents before its publication and these consultations were made by the Irish as well as by the British government.

The document went further than any previous British government in recognising nationalist rights in regard to self-determination: 'The British government agree that it is for the people of Ireland as a whole, by agreement between the two parts respectively, to exercise their right of self-determination on the basis of consent, freely and concurrently given north and south, to bring about a united Ireland, if that is their wish' (para 4). The British will introduce legislation to give effect to any agreement 'on the future relationships in Ireland which the people living in Ireland may themselves so determine without external impediment.' The document also reaffirmed the 1990 statement of Peter Brooke as Secretary of State that the British government 'have no selfish strategic or economic interest in Northern Ireland.'[4]

The most significant change in the British government's position was on self-determination. They are now willing to consider the whole island as the unit for self-determination. In theory this means that they will allow people who are not citizens of the UK (the people of the Republic) to have a say in determining the constitutional status of part of the UK.

However, the principle of majority consent for any change in the status of Northern Ireland was maintained in the document by insisting that the consent of both parts of the island would be required for any constitutional change.

It is difficult in practice to see how any British government can avoid insisting on this. Otherwise they place themselves in a situation where they might have to expel a section of the UK against the will of the majority of the people of that section. That would lead to a break up of the UK.

Secondly, as Albert Reynolds pointed out, the particular mechanism used by the Declaration to work out what self-determination means – namely that any change requires the approval of both the majority in the north and in the south – is not unique. A similar process was used in the unification of Germany, where the consent of both east and west was required.

Thirdly, the Declaration was arguably in accordance with the statement issued by John Hume and Gerry Adams in April 1993: 'We accept that the Irish people as a whole have a right to national self-determination. This is a view shared by a majority of the people of this island though not by all its people. The exercise of self-determination is a matter for agreement between the people of Ireland'.[5]

ARTICLES TWO AND THREE

The Declaration contains a commitment by the Irish government to propose changes in Articles Two and Three of the Republic's Constitution, but only in the context of 'an overall settlement', so that there will have to be concessions for nationalists for this to happen.

A central demand of unionists during the 1990-92 talks was for a change in these Articles. The DUP withdrew from the talks because of the lack of movement on this issue and said that the removal of the Articles was a precondition for new talks. Dick Spring, the Republic's Minister for Foreign Affairs in 1993, was reported as being open to changing, but not removing, the Articles.[6]

Article Two says that: 'The national territory consists of the whole island of Ireland, its islands and the territorial seas.'

Article Three says: 'Pending the re-integration of the national territory, and without prejudice to the right of the Parliament and Government established by this Constitution to exercise jurisdiction over the whole of that territory, the laws enacted by that Parliament shall have the like area and extent of application as the laws of Saorstat Éireann and the like extra-territorial effect'.

The problem with Article Two is that it defines the nation in terms of territory and then makes no distinction between the territory of the nation and that of the state. The definition is presented as a matter of fact rather than of belief. Further, while Article Three limits the *de facto* area of jurisdiction to what is now the Republic of Ireland, it maintains a continued legal claim over what is now Northern Ireland.

In 1987 Christopher and Michael McGimpsey challenged the constitutionality of Article One of the Anglo-Irish Agreement in the Irish High Court on the grounds that it was in conflict with Articles Two and Three of the Republic's Constitution. They argued a) that the Agreement established a framework which limited the freedom of the state in its foreign policy towards the UK; and b) that the Agreement conceded the right of the British government to exercise sovereignty in Northern Ireland. When the case was lost, they appealed to the Supreme Court in 1990. Chief Justice Finlay cited Mr Justice Barrington, who in his judgment on the McGimpsey case in the High Court had said that there were two interpretations of these Articles. The first was based on the decision of the Supreme Court in reference to the Criminal Law Jurisdiction Bill (1977 I.R.). This stated that:

'One of the theories held in 1937 by a substantial number of citizens was that a nation as distinct from a State had rights;

that the Irish people living in what is now called the Republic of Ireland and in Northern Ireland together form one nation: that a nation has a right to unity of territory in some form, be it as a unitary or federal State: and that the Government of Ireland Act 1920, though legally binding, was a violation of that national right to unity which was superior to positive law.'[7]

The Supreme Court in 1990 approved this interpretation which is a pithy summary of the difficulties posed by Articles 2 and 3. It shows up in a stark way the problems of using the language of rights in regard to territorial claims of this kind. At root the problem posed by this interpretation is the same as that confronting many conflicts throughout the world: the belief that the 'nation' must be contiguous with the state. Where this belief is dominant, and where there is also disagreement over what constitutes the nation, then there is conflict, because people cannot agree on the boundaries of the state.

What constitutes a nation is in reality a matter of belief by those who make up its members. Its boundaries cannot be proved – or disproved – by any objective criteria. The 1977 statement is an official statement of what nationalists believe. Unionists believe that Northern Ireland is not part of the Irish nation. In so far as the debate is based on the concept of nationhood, and when the assumption is that nationhood confers a right to unity of territory, no progress can be made.

At the time of the IRA ceasefire in 1994 the issue of consent was still central in political negotiations. But, given the support for the Downing Street Declaration – and it was supported by all political parties north and south – with the exception of Sinn Féin, the DUP, and possibly the UUP – the vast majority of Irish nationalists had moved to a position where, however reluctantly, they seemed willing to accept the principle of consent as outlined in the Declaration.[8] But, given that any changes in Articles Two and Three require a referendum, it would be naïve to assume that any alterations will be made without major debate, both north and south. The key issue for nationalists was two-fold: what returns would they get for this concession in terms both of respect for nationalist identity within Northern Ireland and of north-south structures? Secondly, what changes would be made in political structures within Northern Ireland to ensure greater justice for nationalists, especially in the key areas of job distribution and policing?

Unionist and nationalist vetoes
and the role of the British government

Sinn Féin reject the view that unionist consent is required to bring about a united Ireland and also the analysis of the SDLP that the problem lies in the 'totality of relationships' rather than simply in the presence of the British in Ireland. Further, they reject the British government's position which suggests that the responsibility for dismantling partition lies with Irish nationalists, who, if they wished, could persuade unionists to accept unity.

In 1980 the SDLP, like Sinn Féin, saw the British guarantee as the basis of unionist intransigence. Party leader, John Hume, argued that 'While this guarantee exists there is no incentive for unionists to enter into genuine dialogue with those with whom they share the island of Ireland'.[9] He believed the failure of the British to stand up to the Loyalist strike in 1974 reinforced unionists' beliefs in their ability to withstand any change in British policy. Britain created Northern Ireland, he said, is in charge of Northern Ireland, and 'cannot now be regarded as a remote and benign referee whose well-intentioned whistle the participants no longer hear in the din of conflict. Britain is as responsible today for our ills as she was in 1921 and there will be no resolution until she, like us, takes a new view of the interests of all of us'.[10]

However, after the signing of the Anglo-Irish Agreement in 1985 Hume believed that the British were now neutral. 'By declaring that they will accept the wishes of the people of Northern Ireland, whether those wishes are for union or unity, the British government have declared themselves neutral in the basic quarrel between us; that is a significant advance.'

This argument was crucial in the Hume-Adams dialogue in 1988 and again in 1992. If, Hume argued, the British were neutral, then the only block to unity was lack of agreement among the people living on the island. This meant that republicans were not fighting the British in reality, but unionists.

Sinn Féin refused to accept this position which was why they rejected the principle of consent in the Downing Street Declaration. There were in fact two unionist vetoes under discussion. One was a veto over any constitutional change. The second was a veto over changes in the political structures of Northern Ireland and north-south relationships. Sinn Féin recognised neither. But arguably once the IRA had declared a ceasefire they accepted that they could not impose their views on either the British or the rest of the people on the island. The SDLP, along with the Irish government, in practice accepted the unionist veto over constitutional change, as long as they were the majority, but did not accept that they had any veto over political change. This position was accepted by the British government.

However, the unionists are not the only ones with a veto. Nationalists also have a veto over any changes to the Anglo-Irish Agreement. For unionists the Agreement was the fulfilment of their worst nightmares: the Dublin government was given a role over Northern Ireland. Further, because of the ambiguity of the wording, they believed it was a conspiracy by the British government to expel Northern Ireland from the UK. The claim by Dublin politicians that the Agreement constituted 'almost joint authority' led Peter Robinson to say that Northern Ireland was 'on the windowledge of the union'.[11]

The Agreement changed the balance of power within Northern Ireland. Once it was signed it could only be changed with the consent of both governments. It would be difficult – but not totally impossible – for the south to agree to any changes without the support, or at least the tolerance of the SDLP. What this means is that in any negotiations it is relatively easy for the SDLP to sit back and say 'what we have we hold'. If unionists want to see the Agreement changed then they need to come up with something that is more attractive to the SDLP. But that could only be something that either increased Dublin involvement, or else maintained the level of involvement contained in the Agreement, and at the same time gave nationalists a strong degree of power-sharing. These were major stumbling blocks in the 1990-1992 negotiations. By 1994, however, unionist opposition to the Agreement seemed to have eased: not to the point of accepting it, but of seeing it as a political reality. That, of course, is precisely what the Agreement was. The conference set up by the Agreement was given power to deal with political, security and legal matters, and with cross-border cooperation. Unionists argued that this placed a limit on the authority of the British government. In fact Article 2b explicitly addressed this point: 'There is no derogation from the sovereignty of either the UK government or the Irish government, and each retains responsibility for the decisions and administration of government within its own jurisdiction.' This clause makes clear that the Agreement did not amount to joint authority or 'almost joint authority'. The British government alone retains decision-making authority over Northern Ireland. If there is agreement among the parties within Northern Ireland a devolved executive may be set up, but the Irish government is given no executive role whatever.

The Agreement has introduced another difference in the balance between the two communities. It allows the Irish government to put forward views and proposals on behalf of the minority community. (It will be interesting to see what happens this clause when, and if, nationalists become a majority, which demographers suggest may happen sometime between 2030 and 2050. Will the Irish government then be legally bound to represent unionists and not nationalists?) For unionists this means that where nationalists have a sovereign government to speak on their behalf, they do not. It might be argued that the UK government should and does fulfil this role but there are two arguments against this. One is that the UK is the sovereign government for the whole of Northern Ireland. As such, its concern should be for all the citizens of Northern Ireland, irrespective of their national or political identity.[12] Secondly, unionists, especially after the Agreement was imposed on them, very often do not trust the British government to act on their behalf. An exception to this was the period of the very close relationship that developed between Jim Molyneaux and John Major from 1992 on. This was helped by the Tories' need for unionist support because of their small parliamentary majority. Arthur Aughey makes a good point that in giving the right to the Irish government to represent Northern nationalists and not Northern unionists, the Agreement in fact makes Irish nationalism sectarian.[13]

The Agreement was made between the two governments as a response to the failure of the communities within Northern Ireland to reach agreement on political structures. Despite the fudge in Article One, it marked a major change for the better in the relationship between the two governments. From 1985 on, both governments have worked together on the Northern Ireland problem. Whatever differences there have been between them have been handled within the context of the Agreement. The key task after the 1994 ceasefires was to see if consent could be reached on new political institutions to replace the Agreement. As part of this process John Major announced in September 1994 that any agreement between the political parties would be made subject to a referendum in Northern Ireland. Albert Reynolds said that the south would also hold a referendum to verify any new agreement. The purpose of Major's announcement was to reassure unionists that there had been no secret deal leading up to the IRA ceasefire, but the result of it was to give unionists an effective veto over political as well as constitutional issues. The question was also raised by Peter Robinson of the DUP as to what action the two governments would take in the event of a failure of the Northern Ireland parties to agree. Would they implement a new agreement over their heads?

The question illustrates the difficulty of getting a balanced settlement, or one that sufficient people will regard as balanced. The nationalist agenda in 1994, at least in the mind of the SDLP, seemed to be to develop strong north-south institutional links and to maintain the relationship between the two governments established under the Anglo-Irish Agreement. But Peter Robinson's question was valid. If north-south institutions were developed would it be with the agreement of any new devolved parliament to be set up? Of necessity, any such agreement would require the consent of unionists. But failing such agreement, would the two governments, acting independently of the Northern Ireland parties, set up their own structures, and in any such structures would the Irish government have an increased say? The possibility that this might happen brought a degree of pressure on unionists to come to agreement with the nationalists. The possibility that it might not happen must surely have made it more difficult for republicans to maintain the ceasefire.

POLITICAL STRUCTURES

Both the SDLP and Sinn Féin reject an 'internal settlement'. In a frequently publicised analysis, John Hume defines the conflict in terms of three relationships: between the Unionists and the rest of the island; between Ireland and Britain, and between the parties within Northern Ireland. Of these the most important in his view is the first.

Devolution on its own will not work, in Hume's view, because it fails to face up to the central problem which is the relationship of unionists with the rest of the island. Secondly, he argues that proposals for devolution attempt to deal with only one aspect of the problem, and this is impossible. Agreement has to be reached on all the different pieces of the jigsaw before any new agreement is possible. For this, certain principles should govern the relationship between the two governments. Some principles have already been agreed by the two governments.

The Preamble to the Anglo-Irish Agreement was a very important statement of these. It is not well known, so it is worth while summarising its main provisions here. As a blueprint it remains valid nine years later.

Clause One recognises the relationship between the two countries as unique. It is unique in the number of Irish people living in

Britain, the lack of any requirement for Irish people to have permits to work or vote in Britain, or to have passports to enter Britain, the number of Irish people who have served in British armies during the two world wars, the long history of conflict between the two countries and the shared problem of Northern Ireland.

Clause Two recognises the major interest of both countries in reducing the divisions in Northern Ireland and achieving lasting peace and stability. The interest of Britain in this is obvious. The annual cost to the British exchequer of security in Northern Ireland before the 1994 ceasefires was in excess of £3 billion. The British government have introduced a legal system that is challenged the world over because of its departure from recognised conventional legal practice. It has lost British soldiers and civilians in the conflict. It has suffered heavily from the damage inflicted by IRA bombs in London and elsewhere. For the Irish government the cost of border-related security was higher per capita. It has suffered diplomatic damage through the burning of the British embassy in Dublin and the murder of a British ambassador. It has faced divisions within the country over its northern policy and also over issues such as extradition.

Clause Three recognises 'the need for continuing efforts to reconcile and to acknowledge the rights of the two major traditions that exist in Ireland' and it also recognises and respects the identities of the two communities in Northern Ireland. This is the language of the 1984 Forum. Like the Forum, it lacks any clarification of what the rights of the two traditions are and how they can be reconciled, given that they are contradictory in their full expression. It is of course also a simplification. There are far more than two traditions in the country. But it might have been useful if the clause had mentioned three rather than two: northern unionists, northern nationalists, and the people of the south. As it stands, it suggests that northern and southern nationalists are a monolith, which not only is a major oversimplification, but also heightens the fears of unionists.

Clause Four reaffirms the total rejection by the two governments of any attempt to promote political objectives by violence or the threat of violence 'and their determination to work together to ensure that those who adopt or support such methods do not succeed'. It has been argued that this clause should be an added guarantee to unionists that the status of Northern Ireland will not be changed without their consent.[14]

Clause Five recognises that a condition of genuine reconciliation is that each of the two communities within Northern Ireland recognises and accepts the other's rights.

Clause Six recognises and respects the identities of the two communities in Northern Ireland, 'and the right of each to pursue its aspirations by peaceful and constitutional means'.

Clause Seven commits both governments to work for a society in Northern Ireland in which all 'may live in peace, free from discrimination and intolerance, and with the opportunity for both communities to participate fully in the structures and processes of government'.

In practice, there are three main areas of contention in relation to political structures. One is the issue of a power-sharing executive. A second is north-south structures, and the third is that of security. By 1994 unionists seemed to be moving towards accepting power-sharing. But it was not clear whether they wanted major or minor powers for any new devolved Northern Ireland executive. Secondly, it was unclear how much power they were willing to give to nationalists in practice.

From a nationalist point of view, the proposals for north-south structures in tourism, inward investment and agriculture, while important economically, were not so significant in terms of identity.

The issue of security was much more contentious.

THE ISSUE OF SECURITY

Security had come up in the 1990-92 inter-party talks. The SDLP had reportedly brought forward a paper on the issue, but it was not presented to the talks because the Irish government did not accept it. This was because it contained a clause calling for a 'hot pursuit' territory on both sides of the border.

The Anglo-Irish Agreement had previously attempted to deal with security and at the time of the ceasefire it was its provisions that governed relations between the two governments in this area. For the British government, the key motive for signing the Agreement was the prospect of greater cross-border security co-operation. This in turn raised a question about the extent to which the Irish government had been committed to doing all in their power to deal with paramilitary activity prior to the Agreement. They argued that they were doing what they could, but that the Agreement would give greater facility for structural co-operation between the two governments and their respective security forces. The Agreement has been successful in damage-limitation in regard to disputes between the two governments over security issues. Part of the reason for this is that information about what has happened in incidents – or at least the British government's version of it – is now made available speedily to the Irish government.

Secondly, the fact that the Irish government can raise such incidents at meetings of the conference, and call for special meetings if they wish to, allows it to give the impression that they are doing something practical about the incidents.

Thirdly, there is at least a degree of psychological pressure brought to bear on the British government when they are questioned about security incidents. This is better than nothing. Its effect is, however, clearly limited in cases where the SAS, or other undercover security force personnel have been used to kill paramilitaries. The investigation of such incidents is done by the Northern Ireland security forces, acting on behalf of the British government. Until greater oversight is conducted by more independent agencies it will be impossible not to view the results of any enquiries with a great degree of suspicion.

Article 7c states that 'there is a need for a programme of special measures in Northern Ireland to improve relations between the security forces and the community, with the object in particular of making the security forces more readily accepted by the nationalist community'.

One of the greatest weaknesses of the Agreement lies in this clause. Security is the most important issue facing people living in a divided community. This clause comes nowhere near to answering the problem. It leaves the authority of the RUC and the British army untouched. At the very least it should have been possible to increase the power of the Police Authority, particularly by giving its members, rather than the Chief Constable, the power to decide what constitutes 'policy' and what constitutes 'operational' matters. Under Article 6, the Irish government has the right to suggest nominees for the Police Authority. Such a right is of limited use unless the Authority has proper powers.

The European Context

Europe has been important to the SDLP for several reasons. One is John Hume's own experience. He has served as an MEP since 1979 and has seen at first hand the benefits that can be wrung from the EU, although its contribution is well below the net input of the UK government. He has also played a major role, along with Ian Paisley, in getting these benefits for Northern Ireland. Secondly, Europe is attractive as a means of reducing the symbolism of British domination. Thirdly, the notion of a Europe of the regions is attractive for both economic and political reasons.

The European Union is sometimes seen as a structure with which both sides can identify. In practice, however, unionists have had great difficulty in identifying with Europe. They see it as Catholic in its emphasis (this is particularly true of the DUP) and they suspect that any closer connections with Europe would help nationalists more than unionists.

THE QUESTION OF MINORITIES

Pluralism and the Catholic Church

A major theme in the area of minority rights has been that of pluralism. The Catholic Church's position on this has been influenced by changes in its understanding of how it should relate with secular society. Liam Ryan points to a major change in papal encyclicals starting with John XXIII. Before that, Irish bishops, in keeping with the tone of papal teaching, were authoritarian. With *Mater et Magistra* of John XXIII there enters a note of humility, a sense that the church does not have all the answers.[15] But this has not been a consistent move. On the one hand bishops have admitted the right of Catholics to disagree with them in conscience. They have also accepted that 'There are many things which the Catholic Church holds to be morally wrong and no one has ever suggested, least of all the church herself, that they should be prohibited by the state.'[16]

On the other hand, they have vigorously opposed efforts to change the constitutional ban on divorce. There are two reasons why the divorce debate is important to the Northern conflict. One is that many argue that if the south could become more pluralist the option of a united Ireland would then be more attractive to unionists. Secondly, many in the south are committed to the liberalisation of family-issue laws within the Republic as part of the effort to get a greater separation of church and state, and also to take account of the need for a greater pluralism. Divorce was a major issue in the debates at the New Ireland Forum in 1984. (This body should be distinguished from the Forum for Peace and Reconciliation which the Taoiseach undertook to set up under the Downing Street Declaration.) It was difficult at times to tell when members of the Forum were primarily motivated by the liberal agenda and when they were dominated by the nationalist one.

The meeting between the members of the Forum and the Catholic bishops was an important moment in the movement of southern society towards greater independence of the hierarchy.

For the first time the bishops were cross-examined in public by politicians from all the main parties about the effects their religious positions had on politics.[17] The process itself contributed much to the demystification of the role of bishops in Irish politics. The confrontation – the term used by John Kelly – between the members of the Forum and the representatives of the Irish Catholic hierarchy was also a graphic illustration of the extent to which society in the south was moving out firmly, if still somewhat fitfully, from under the umbrella of the leaders of the Catholic Church.

In their questions at the Forum, the politicians made two major criticisms. One was that the bishops' position did not take proper account of the minority Protestant group within the south. To this the bishops replied that majorities also have rights and where the overwhelming proportion of the people were Catholic their view should prevail. If there were a united Ireland, that would change the situation because the number of Protestants would increase. John Kelly of Fine Gael saw this as little comfort for his Protestant constituents in Dublin. Seamus Mallon of the SDLP asked if northern Catholics were any worse in their personal morals because of the availability of divorce in Northern Ireland.

Ultimately no satisfactory answer to the problem of minorities was given by the bishops, but what the discussion exposed was that no such answer exists. Where one draws the line between public and private morality is a necessarily shifting line in any society. In practice the size, unity, and political influence of a minority is crucial in determining the amount any government will allow the legislature to be influenced by their moral requirements.

The Forum also discussed mixed marriages because some members saw the Catholic Church's laws on mixed marriages as a block to reconciliation.[18] The main issue was the promise required of the Catholic partner to do all in their power to bring the children of a mixed marriage up as Catholics. Bishop Cassidy said that the bishops had considered seeking a derogation from this rule from Rome. After some consideration they had decided against doing so because they believed that it would have had no chance of success. To do so would therefore have been a mere political exercise. 'But', he added, 'You can take it that if there is anything in that area we can do to further reconciliation, we will do it.'

In the case of both divorce and mixed marriages, changes in the civil law or in the laws of the Catholic Church would have made a positive contribution to reconciliation. The change would not have been dramatic. Unionists would certainly not have sought unity with the south. But such changes could have been elements in the slow build up of trust that is so desperately needed between the different communities on this island. The issue of divorce raises questions about our priorities: is it more important to protect the family unity in society – assuming the ban on divorce helps this? Or is it more important to let the ban go, because reconciliation is a priority? However, if we choose the latter option, we are also making an assumption, namely, that removing the ban will make an important impact on reconciliation.

The treatment of economically deprived people

The SDLP is often criticised for its failure to extend its class base. It has been strongest in rural, middle-class, Catholic areas. The party has made a significant effort to change this by targeting west Belfast in the 1992 general election where Joe Hendron was successful in defeating Gerry Adams, albeit with the help of some Protestant voters who decided that the SDLP were less objectionable from their point of view than Sinn Féin. They have also made important links in Portadown with a local economic and community development group, Drumcree Cooperative. In Derry and Newry the party also has good links with local groups.

However, the party's organisation in many areas is still weak. Sinn Féin has often proved itself more effective in giving the impression that they were better at handling local political issues. But up to the ceasefire their contribution went hand-in-hand with the IRA bombing campaign which led to massive loss of investment and therefore of jobs.

The issue of involving different classes in politics also highlights the need for a devolved government, not only with power-sharing but also with a proportional representational type voting. If such a system were in place then there would be some meaning to local politics in Northern Ireland. As it is, political structures are confined to local councils that have very little power, or to the Westminster Parliament which has power but which is appointed on the basis of crude majority voting. People are unlikely to take part in politics unless they believe in the possibility of being elected to bodies that can make some effective decisions.

CONCLUSION

At the end of this survey of Irish nationalism at the time of the 1994 ceasefire, what are the main themes that have emerged?

One is that there are questions about the usefulness of the idea of a nation state and these need to be faced.

A second is that the issue of consent has not yet been resolved. There has been movement from 1980 so that now all the nationalist parties, with the exception of Sinn Féin, are committed to accepting the principle of consent as outlined in the Downing Street Declaration. However, this is an intergovernmental statement, it lacks the status of the Anglo-Irish Agreement which is an international treaty, and Article One of the Agreement is a fudge. I discussed the issue of Articles Two and Three of the Irish Constitution and noted that Fianna Fáil are committed to seeking approval in a referendum to change them, when circumstances are right.

By the right circumstances is presumably meant satisfactory changes in political structures within Northern Ireland and between north and south, from the point of view of nationalists. In the political battle that must ensue over these issues I suggested that both nationalists and unionists have an effective veto: unionists because, as the majority, they will have the opportunity to reject any political settlement in a referendum; nationalists because they can fall back on the Anglo-Irish Agreement, unless they are offered something more appealing to them.

The period from 1984 marks a very great development in Irish nationalism. The Forum Report and the Anglo-Irish Agreement received wide support among nationalists with the exception of the paramilitaries, and the Declaration was enthusiastically received in the south, and among many northern nationalists. The documents show a movement towards facing up to the reality of the existence of 900,000 unionists on the island and the impossibility of imposing a united Ireland against their will. But they also show a greater openness to reconciliation and an awareness that any militarily imposed solution, even it were possible, would not be desirable. Further, there is a huge development from the stance of many Fianna Fáil deputies at the Forum where the stress was on Northern Ireland being a 'failed political entity', to that of the Declaration where it is accepted by the leader of Fianna Fáil that there will be no change in the north's constitutional status without majority approval.

The period also shows a development in the British stance. It is a far cry from Mrs Thatcher's 1981 statement that Northern Ireland is as British as any part of the UK to that of the Declaration that the people of Ireland as a whole have the right to self-determination without outside interference.

What this shows is that, at the level of the two governments, a significant degree of political reconciliation has taken place. This is of crucial importance in the conflict as a whole. It is the two governments that set the context within which the violence has taken place. It is the ambiguities in their relationship that fuelled the fears and uncertainties within the groups in Northern Ireland. The three documents show a progressive move to rid the intergovernmental relationship of such ambiguities.

The movement at the constitutional level has not been matched by similar moves at a political level. In Northern Ireland civil rights remain extremely insecure. This in part has been due to the violence of the paramilitaries, but it is also due to the unjustifiable powers that central government has taken to itself, and to the lack of a proper constitution. Secondly, the accountability of the security forces remains unsatisfactory. Thirdly, there is as yet no agreement on two major issues: a power-sharing executive for Northern Ireland, and north-south political structures.

Behind these constitutional and political issues lie some faith questions: what sort of faith do we bring to our political dilemmas? In what way do we view our political opponents? When we speak of community in Northern Ireland we quite properly refer at times to groups that can be distinguished by their history, feelings and relationships. But how much are we aware of our calling to be part of another deeper community that includes everyone in Ireland, north and south?

Notes:
1 *Scenario for peace*, p 2.
2 *ibid*, p 3.
3 New Ireland Forum, Public Session No 11, 19 Jan 1984, p 27.
4 9 November 1990, reported *The Irish Times*, 10 November 1990.
5 *The Irish Times*, 26 April 1993.
6 *The Irish Times*, 11 February 1993.
7 Ken Maginnis, *McGimpsey and McGimpsey v Ireland*, Dungannon: 1990.
8 A poll in October 1994 showed that 83% of the people of the south wanted a united Ireland, but 75% accepted the principle of consent.
9 John Hume, *The Irish Times*, 21 May 1980, p 10.
10 John Hume, Talk in St Anne's Cathedral, Belfast, 3 March 1982, *cf The Irish Times*, 4 March 1982, p 14.
11 *Belfast Newsletter*, 26 November 1985.
12 Aughey, op. cit., is good on this point.
13 Aughey, op. cit., p. 54.

14 Council on Social Welfare of the Methodist Church in Ireland, *The Anglo-Irish Agreement*, Appendix A: 'The Anglo-Irish Agreement, A Study Paper', 23 December 1985, p 17.

15 Liam Ryan, 'Church and politics: the last twenty-five years', *The Furrow*, Vol 30, 1979, pp 3-25.

16 Statement of the Irish hierarchy, *The Irish Times*, 26 November 1973.

17 New Ireland Forum, 9 February 1984.

18 During my own meeting with the Forum (4 October 1983) this was the first issue about which I was questioned.

SECTION II

God is a God of Community

At this point in our analysis we need to shift gear. In the second section we will look at some scriptural themes that are relevant. The material we will be considering is obviously going to be quite different from the political issues that we have been considering. But the important question for the reader, as we go through the biblical section, will be: can any of these themes be brought to bear usefully on our situation in Ireland?

CHAPTER 3

The Three Persons who liberate

Like all Christians, Catholics take their primary inspiration from the story of God, and of God's Son, that unfolds in the scriptures and in the tradition of the church. In that story we learn much about who the Christian God is, about how the Jewish people – who are still God's Chosen People – understood their relationship with God, the implications this had for the way they lived, and the things that matter to Jesus whom Christians came to believe was God's anointed Son.

One of the key questions in theology is 'Who is God?' All of us have an implicit answer. Because our idea of God is implicit and because we are often not fully aware of what we think about God, we can be misled by false assumptions.

In this chapter I want to suggest that we need a far greater stress on the fact that God is three persons, living in a perfect community, and on the God who liberates his people from oppression.

I believe that if we stressed these characteristics of God, our politics would be different. We would place a greater emphasis on the building of community. This means, not that we rule out constructive conflict, but that we raise questions about issues of justice, that we take much greater responsibility for the world and the people in it whom God has placed in our hands, that we cope better with suffering and failure, and that we engage in a radical reshaping both of the church and of society in line with some elements of the feminist critique.

God as a community of three persons

One of the central things that Jesus revealed to us is that God is Three Persons. But this has often been downplayed in our understanding of God. As Karl Rahner says 'Christians, for all their orthodox profession of faith in the Trinity, are almost just monotheist in their actual religious existence'.[1] Too often we have been unitarians. We have seen God as one person.

The church went through a tortuous route to articulate the

48

dogma of the Trinity. But at the end of that journey it was clear that the Holy Spirit, while being the Spirit of Jesus, was a distinct person, and that the Son was a distinct person from the Father. Yet God was still one.

This led to questions about the relationships between the three Persons. It is here that the dogma of the Trinity is particularly important for us today. It is beyond our imagination to conceive of three persons who are one. Modern western society, in particular, has placed an enormous stress on the individual. We define individuals as essentially separate beings. That is correct, but what we tend to underplay is the context within which all of us become individuals. That context is society. John Donne's line 'No man is an island' is not simply a pious aspiration. It is a statement of fact that as individuals we can only exist in relation to a collective society.

What the doctrine of the Trinity tells us is that our God, on whom we are modelled, is three distinct persons, but whose relationships with each other are so filled with respect, excitement, other-directedness, commitment, caring, and passion, that they are one in nature.

Karl Rahner says somewhere that in heaven we will finally realise that God is mystery. By this he means that we often tend to assume that once we get to the next life and see God face to face, that will be that. We will have nothing else to learn. That makes heaven seem rather boring. Rahner's point is that, on the contrary, we will be caught up in the three Persons who will for ever be mysteries: mysteries in the sense that the wonder of their being will never be exhausted. What we may also realise is that we ourselves are mystery: that the wonder of our beings will never be exhausted; that we are really made in the image of God. Heaven, then, will be about discovering the ever newness not only of the three Persons, but also of each other, partly as individuals but more importantly as a new community.

We are made in the image of God. If we understand God to be three Persons whose relationships are the most important thing that we know about them, then we need to understand ourselves also primarily in terms of relationships. For Christians the basic model of society cannot therefore be one of individuals living as separate atoms, but rather of peoples living in diversity, with different cultures, languages, skills and histories, but also capable not only of accepting, but of loving, each other. The Christian community will therefore see diversity not as a threat, but as an opportunity to look for the mystery that exists in other communities, to search for God not only in the familiar, but also in what is different. Churches that are self-contained, that have no urgency in searching for the God that lies beyond their own boundaries, are not sharing in the mystery of the Trinity. They are living with a God that does not exist.

The doctrine of the Trinity is a fundamental challenge to Irish and British Christians. If we cannot build community with each other we cannot be in community with God.

GOD THE LIBERATOR
The Covenant and the Exodus

The exodus was the central event in the self-understanding of the Jewish people. Generation after generation were told the story of how God had liberated his people under the leadership of Moses from the slavery of the Pharaohs. Israel was chosen from among all the nations by God for this act of freedom, and as the Chosen People she is to be set up in the new land of Canaan, which will be flowing with milk and honey. It is the moment in history when God shows himself as a loving father to his people. It is also a pledge of the people's future salvation to which they will look back during the time of the captivity in Babylon and in their conflicts with the Assyrians. It is the basis of their trust in God. The event was celebrated in the central act of worship of the people: the Passover meal, which Jesus held with his disciples the night before his death. In the New Testament Jesus will be seen as the new Paschal Lamb who is sacrificed to save his people.

The Exodus story gives a picture of a God who is utterly involved in the life and struggles of his people. There is no hint here of a distant God – although the transcendence of God is emphasised – or of a God who shuns conflict. The anger of God against oppressors is revealed. But it is not passive anger: Yahweh intervenes on behalf of his people who are being oppressed.

The exodus experience is also central to the covenant, or agreement, which God made with his people on Mount Sinai: he will be their God and they will be his people. On God's side this means that he will protect and rescue the people. On their side it means that they worship him before all other Gods and obey the law. Central to this is social justice: failure to treat others in the community properly in itself removes a person from the community. The God who rescued his people from slavery in Egypt will not tolerate them acting in an oppressive way towards each other. 'Therefore because you trample upon the poor and take from him exactions of wheat, you have built houses of hewn stone, but you shall not dwell in them;

you have planted pleasant vineyards, but you shall not drink their wine' (Amos 5:11 RSV). The laws of the community are placed in the ark of the covenant and this is the meeting place between God and the people. The worship of the people is thus linked both to their first experience of liberation from Egypt, and to respect for the law which governs their social relationships.

The covenant is central to the teaching of the prophets. They see the catastrophes which fall on the people as signs of the judgement of God on them for failing to keep their side of the covenant. Thus Jeremiah promised the people defeat at the hands of their enemies because of their unfaithfulness. This is the 'angry' God of the Hebrew scriptures. God was angry because his people were oppressed. But the Hebrew scriptures present God's anger or judgement as something that the people draw down on themselves by oppressing others. They thereby remove themselves from the covenant community.

The prophets also used images of human love to draw out the deeper meaning of the covenant. Yahweh is seen as the lover, the father, the mother, the shepherd, and the vinedresser. Although the people constantly break the covenant, the prophets promise that God will make a new covenant with them in which once again Yahweh will be their God and they will be his people.

The story of the exodus has been an inspiration for liberation theologians. For many it is the basic scriptural text. It is seen as the prototype for the liberation needed by so many oppressed groups in the world today. It is an example of God calling, choosing and rescuing those who are oppressed. But it is also an image of an oppressed people responding together to this call, and thereby refusing to accept their oppression passively. It is a picture of the way God sides with the deprived in history: there is no question of God being neutral between the Egyptians and the Jews in the story. So also in today's world there is no hint of a God who is neutral between oppressor and oppressed. This does not mean that God hates the oppressor, but he is angry with him and is opposed to him. An analogy is a mother with two sons, one of whom is bullying the other. The mother loves both, but she will oppose the bully.

The exodus story is the very antithesis of a God who deals primarily with the individual rather than with the people as a community, or of a God who is essentially concerned about spiritual matters and is therefore uninvolved in the suffering of people in this life. In Ireland, both north and south, neither the exodus nor the covenant are theological motifs that make a major impact on the life of large groups in the Catholic Church. For example, there is no comparison between their impact and the stress placed in popular religion on the intercession of the saints, especially Mary, or on Lourdes or Knock. In both of these shrines of pilgrimage there is an emphasis on liberation: they are places of incredible support for many who are sick, and they can lead to cures, both psychological and physical. They also play an important role in building a sense of community in Catholic parishes and dioceses. But there is also something in the story of God that we have received about taking responsibility for our political future; that the northern conflict is in part made by Catholics and Protestants, north and south of the border; that we therefore have a possibility and a responsibility to contribute something to its solution. The spirituality of Lourdes and Knock is not centred on these issues.

The Exodus myth inspired the Jewish people to think in terms of their liberation as a people. It allowed them to see God as someone intimately involved with their lives as a people. It could play a similar role in Ireland if it was reflected on in a way that is constructive.

Certainly, if the exodus and the covenant motifs became more prominent in the right way in the thinking of Catholic Church groups, and if the notion of community contained in them were extended to include the different groups on this island, then the church would be in a much stronger position to raise serious questions for society.

Of course, emphasising the exodus and the covenant would not have this effect if it were done in the wrong way. In many fundamentalist Protestant Churches these themes are used to show that the particular church or group has been specially chosen by God, that they are different from other men and women because of this – and better than them – and that, as a result, other Christian communities are not in contact with God.

Using these themes in this way is to use them as sociological devices to protect an insecure community from the perils of entering into relationship with the real world. It is also to misunderstand the call that the God of community is giving to his people in these scriptural events. That call is not only to live and act as a community themselves, but to be open to making community with all other people. This interpretation of the events is of course based on salvation history as it is now available to us, not as it was to the scriptural writers of the original events. That history now includes the life of Jesus, and the struggles in the early church to understand that non-Jewish people, the Gentiles, were also called to be part of God's community.[2]

It is worth noting that Dick Spring, leader of the Labour Party in the Republic, made the suggestion of making a new *covenant* while he was Tánaiste in 1993. The covenant would guarantee fundamental rights to any group that finds itself in a minority, thus applying to the nationalists in the first instance, but also to unionists if they become a minority in the future.[3]

The theme of liberation is continued in the New Testament story of Jesus.

JESUS' MISSION

In the gospel accounts of the mission of Jesus, especially in Luke, the poor are the most important people in God's community. If intimacy with the Father was one aspect of Christ's mission that upset his listeners, this was a second. Jesus put the poor at centre stage in the community. 'Blessed are the poor, for theirs is the kingdom of heaven' (Lk 6).

Luke opens his account of Jesus' ministry with a statement about his mission: In his first sermon to be reported in the gospel Jesus quotes Isaiah 61:

The Spirit of the Lord is upon me,

Because he has anointed me to bring good news to the poor.

He has sent me to proclaim release to the captives and recovery of sight to the blind,

To set at liberty those who are oppressed,

To proclaim the acceptable year of the Lord (Lk 4:18 ff).

'Today', he tells his hearers, 'this scripture has been fulfilled in your hearing.' The poor, those who suffer, and prisoners, are put at the centre of the stage. This happens again in the beatitudes, and also in the incident where John the Baptist sends messengers to ask Jesus if he is the Messiah. John had preached a vengeful God, but Jesus is the messenger of mercy. His practice of eating with sinners challenged the wrath of God that John expected. Jesus responds by saying: 'Go back and tell John what you are hearing and seeing: the blind can see, the lame can walk, those who suffer from dreaded skin diseases are made clean, the deaf hear, the dead are brought back to life, and the good news is preached to the poor' (Mt 11:4).[4]

The context in which Jesus was preaching was one in which Jewish religion had very clear answers to two questions. One was 'How can I enter the kingdom of God?' and the second was 'Who will be a member of the kingdom of God?'[5]

For the Pharisees the answer to the first question was that one became part of God's community by keeping the law. This contained thousands of detailed prescriptions for every aspect of life. In order to know these laws one had to study them, and without knowing them it was impossible to keep them. This meant the poor were excluded from God's community, because not having the financial wherewithal to study the law they were incapable of keeping it. This made them unclean and put them outside God's community – in the view of the Pharisees.

Jesus proposed a radically different answer to the two questions. For him the only way one could enter God's community was by showing compassion to those in need, by helping them to become liberated.

The oppressed

The most obvious place where Jesus proposed the first part of this teaching on compassion is in the Last Judgement scene in Matthew 25. Matthew gives the story a special solemnity by speaking of the Lord coming in glory surrounded by his angels and taking his seat on his throne of glory. He repeats the message of the story four times: that those who enter God's community will do so because 'whatever you did to the least of these my brethren you did to me.' Similarly, those who are excluded find themselves in that position because 'I was hungry and you did not feed me ...'

Secondly, in the story of Dives and Lazarus (Lk 16:19 ff) the rich man ends up in Hades, not because of anything he did, but because he did nothing. There is no suggestion in the story that the rich man is the cause of the poor man's situation. For all we know, Lazarus may have drunk himself into poverty, or he may have been the victim of an accident. We are not told. All we know is that the rich man lived in a good house and ate well. Lazarus lived outside his gate and went hungry. Because of that the rich man is excluded from God's community.

What this parable is pointing up is that it is impossible to be part of God's community without working actively to create a human community. God does not exclude the rich man from the community. He excludes himself. He is not in community with Lazarus. He does not see Lazarus as his brother. If he did, Lazarus would not be hungry. The way that he responds – or does not respond – to Lazarus is, according to Jesus, the way that God sees the rich man responding to him. Because he failed to build a relationship with Lazarus the rich man failed to build a relationship with God.

The same message is central to the parable of the Good Samaritan (Lk 10). Once again the priest and the Levite who walked by the injured man did not cause his injuries. That was done by the bandits who robbed him. Further, the injured man was not one of their family, or a relative by marriage, or a business partner, or even someone from their neighbourhood. There are no grounds for assuming they even knew the injured man. But because they did nothing, because they simply walked by on the other side of the road, for that reason the priest and levite are excluded from God's community. They did not show compassion.

A further occasion on which Jesus highlighted the central importance of the poor in God's community was at the wedding feast in Luke 14. At the end of the dinner Jesus tells his host that the next time he has a feast he should invite the poor, the crippled, the lame and the blind, and not his family, relatives and friends. In this way his host will be blessed, because, unlike his relatives, the poor will not be able to pay him back. God will repay him on the last day. Jesus then goes on to tell the parable of the great feast. In this story the host invites various rich people, all of whom make excuses as to why they cannot attend. The excuses are all concerned with money ('I have bought a field and must go and look at it ... I have bought five pairs of oxen and am on my way to try them out', except in the case of Luke who adds the excuse about the wife). Angry at the rejection, the host then sends his servants out to invite the poor, the crippled, the blind and the lame, who are living in 'the streets and alleys of the town'. But there is still more room left over. So the host orders his servants to go out to the country roads and lanes and compel the poor to come in. The poor in this case are outside the town which suggests that they are the Gentiles. 'I tell you all that none of those men who were invited will taste my dinner!'

There are several points in this parable. One is highlighting the conflict between the religious leaders of the day and Jesus: they are excluding themselves from God's community because they do not recognise Jesus. The reason they do not recognise him is because they do not know God. God is a God of compassion, a God in relationship with the poor and the outcasts. Those who do not know this cannot recognise God. If they cannot recognise God they cannot recognise his Son.

The second point is that the poor are compelled to come to the feast in order to fill all the places. One explanation for this is that the likely reaction of deprived people to an invitation like this is simple disbelief. 'Winos' and 'dossers' do not get invited to great feasts by important people. That is why the host tells his servants to compel them to come. Only when they arrive will they realise that this invitation is genuine and not a sick joke at their expense.

Thirdly, the people outside the town are the Gentiles. They are not part of the Chosen People. Yet they also are invited to the feast.[6]

The poor, the sick, the lame, the blind and the Gentiles are all being invited – and coming – into God's community before the scribes and Pharisees. So central are the poor that in a sense they distribute the entrance tickets to heaven. Peter McVerry speaks of the last judgement as the place where God finally reveals his kingdom for what it is: the community that belongs to the poor. Because he is the God of compassion, God can do no other than take those who have been deprived, rejected and pushed aside, and show them his compassion. He brings them into the community, not because they are morally better than anyone else, but as a free gift, because of who he is, because of his compassion. 'God makes a preferential option for these people who are suffering. They are his children, his sons and daughters. Nothing could be more important to the Father than that this suffering be relieved or taken away. Is there anything more important to God than the suffering of his own children?'[7]

In Northern Ireland one of the recurring tensions is that between those working for social justice and those working for political change. The latter argue that there will never be social change without political change. The argument is an old one within Irish nationalism: in 1918 the Labour Party decided to give priority to the national struggle in the hope that socialism would follow. They were to be disappointed. The theory is repeated by some republicans who argue for the necessity of overthrowing the Irish Republic and setting up a socialist state once the British have been removed from Northern Ireland.

The gospels do not tell us what political changes are necessary to bring about justice. At no stage are we told that Jesus addressed the question of the Roman occupation of Palestine, although, as an intelligent and concerned Jew, he would surely have considered the question. What he does point out is that unless a society places a special value on respect for deprived people, then that society will be separated from God because it allows a situation of oppression to continue.

The depressing reality about the political programmes of either nationalists or unionists is that none of them show any likelihood of radically changing the position of deprived people in Northern Ireland. It is politically naïve to believe that, simply because of a change in political structures in one small country, major economic benefits will follow. Political structures are important. But in a worldwide economic system, changes in one country alone are of limited benefit.

If we are to take the gospels seriously then two questions to be addressed by all political groups in Northern Ireland are: in what way are their political proposals likely to benefit those who are living lives of unacceptable economic deprivation? Secondly, how much does it matter if we have a society with a very large gap between the rich and the poor?

Notes:

1 *Theological Investigations 4*, quoted in Gerald A. McCool, *A Rahner Reader*, London: Dartmouth, Longman and Todd, 1975, p 136.

2 *cf* The story of the conversion of Cornelius by Peter in Acts 10. Robin Boyd, former director of the Irish School of Ecumenics, is interesting on his experience as a child in a Presbyterian Church in Northern Ireland being taught how his people were the chosen 'remnant' of God. *cf* Robin Boyd, *Ireland: Christianity discredited or Pilgrim's Progress?*, Geneva: WCC, 1988. 'A favourite texts of fundamentalist preachers is 'Come ye out from among them' (2 Cor 6:17).

3 Address to the Irish Association, 5 March 1993.

4 *cf* John J. O'Donnell, *The Mystery of the Triune God*, London: Sheed & Ward, 1987.

5 In this section I am in part using themes developed by Peter McVerry SJ, in an unpublished talk, Dublin: 1990.

6 C. Stuhlmueller, 'The Gospel according to Luke', in the *Jerome Biblical Commentary*, p 148.

7 McVerry, ibid.

CHAPTER 4

The Son who is
inclusive and reconciling

1. GOD IS INCLUSIVE

The Christian God wants to include all men and women in his community. There are two groups on whom the scriptures, especially the gospels, place great emphasis: women and people who are considered outcasts by society. I want to look briefly at each of these in turn.

THE SCRIPTURES AND THE ROLE OF WOMEN

The deep changes in our understanding of gender roles in society over the past thirty years are one of the factors that have made us look afresh at our models of God. It is not possible here to give a detailed account of the treatment of women in the bible. Some of it is positive and some negative. But it is worth naming some issues that have been raised because a different response to these would open up new and more respectful relationships between men and women in the church. In turn, I believe this would make a profound impact on the way that we do politics.

In this section I want to look at six issues: 1) the way Mary, the relative of Elizabeth, has been seen at times almost on a par with God; 2) feminine as well as masculine attributes of God; 3) Mary as mediatrix of God's grace; 4) Mary's role as a faith companion, as a balance to her role as mother of Jesus; 5) the relationship Jesus had with women, and the role they seem to have played as co-workers in the early church.

The status accorded to Mary

At times the church has suffered from an exaggerated, and at times heretical, devotion to Mary. For example, some people have seen her almost as the equal of God, supplying the feminine qualities that are lacking in God. But many of the qualities ascribed to her – meekness, modesty, submissiveness, silence – have also been used as instruments in society to help keep women subservient to men.

An interesting prayer in this context is the 'Hail, holy, Queen'. It is a beautiful prayer and has a particularly evocative quality when sung in Latin after a funeral. But parts of it are questionable. Take, for example, 'Hail, our life, our sweetness, and our hope!' Mary is not our life, our sweetness and our hope. God is, not Mary. Poetic licence about the role of Mary has at times harmed our understanding of God. The same prayer can be wonderful when it is prayed instead to Our Lord who really is 'our life, our sweetness, and our hope'.

Masculine and feminine in God

A second series of questions has arisen about the way we have tended to give God exclusively 'masculine' virtues. This has led some theologians to stress 'feminine' aspects in God. This has opened up for many a deeper awareness of the tenderness of God, the commitment of God to his people, the passionate love that God has for us.

When speaking about God, the bible frequently uses what have been seen as traditionally feminine virtues. 'For a long time I have held my peace, I have kept still and restrained myself; now I will cry out like a woman in travail, I will gasp and pant' (Is 42:14); 'Can a woman forget her sucking child, that she should have no compassion on the son of her womb? Even if these may forget, yet I will not forget you' (Is 49:15); 'Shall I bring to the birth and not cause to bring forth? says the Lord; shall I, who cause to bring forth, shut the womb? says your God' (Is 66:9).

There is a danger in looking at masculine and feminine descriptions of God that we will simply reinforce traditional stereotypes. However, a scriptural understanding of God should challenge this because it will show God as having all the virtues that we can see in ourselves as both men and women, with strong masculine and feminine elements within each of us. In speaking of the first Person of the Trinity it is not then inappropriate to use the term 'Mother' as well as 'Father', 'she' as well as 'he'.

Mary as mediatrix of grace

A third issue has been that of Mary as mediatrix. In an old example people were told that a child will always go to the mother first when he is looking for something, and get her to approach the father on his behalf. This was then applied to Mary in relation to both Jesus and the Father. The assumption was that we will have a better chance of getting what we pray for by approaching both Jesus and the Father through Mary.

To suggest that somehow we do better by going through saints than by going to God directly can imply – and is often understood as meaning – that God is less approachable, that she understands us less, that she is less tender, loving and passionate than Mary or the other saints.

Protestant reaction to all this has been very negative and nowhere more so than in Northern Ireland. The abuses and exaggerations in the devotion have undermined the credibility of the church's teaching on the true role of Mary. Vatican II refused to declare Mary mediatrix of all graces, and insisted on discussing her role within the context of the *Constitution on the Church*. If this teaching were known more widely, not only would it help to include those women who are alienated by the gender stereotypes associated with the traditional role of Mary; it would also help to break down barriers between Protestant and Catholic Churches.

A proper presentation of Mary restores her – and the saints – to their correct, and very important, place. That place is as part of the community of heaven who are gathered in love around the three Persons. Thus, when we pray, it is highly appropriate to bring to mind the picture of that heavenly community and to join with those who have gone before us – especially the saints that we know – in praising and loving the God whom it is legitimate to address as both our Father and our Mother.

Mary as faith companion as well as mother of Jesus
A fourth issue is the emphasis the church has placed on Mary's role as mother of God. The main references to Mary in the New Testament are all in the infancy narratives. Outside these she is mentioned not more than twice by any of the evangelists. All of them stress her role as a faithful disciple, rather than her role as biological mother. The most obvious reference on this point is Mark 3. His family arrive to take Jesus home because they have been told he is mad. He responds by asking 'Who is my mother? Who are my brothers? ... Whoever does what God wants him to do is my brother, my sister, my mother.'

Claire Murphy points out that the Celtic church emphasised Mary's role as a faith companion to accompany disciples as they walk through life. This was a different emphasis from that on the continent, where the stress on the virgin birth was taught by Ambrose, Augustine, Leo the Great and Jerome. One motive for this may have been that the Fathers of the Church associated the pains of birth with sin. Also, by denying a human father to Jesus, the church could argue that he received his life directly from God. This is because, according to the biology of the time, the woman had no role in the creation of life, other than to be a receptacle for the man's seed. By the fourteenth century the devotion had become sentimentalised, possibly because of the influences of notions of romantic love that then became popular. Marian devotion peaked in the nineteenth and twentieth centuries and was accompanied by a huge number of apparitions of Mary. In Ireland in the 1980s there were many accounts of bleeding and moving statues.

Jesus' relationship with women and their role in the early church
Fifthly, Jesus and at least some parts of the early church included women in ministry in a way that seems very different from their exclusion from our church's ministry today. The way that Jesus included women was part of the way he tried to take all human beings seriously and to treat them with equal respect.

In the New Testament he included women as his friends and co-workers: Mary Magdalene may well have been the person who was closest to him. We are told that women went with him on his journeys, and that it was women who stayed closest to him at the end. He refused to accept traditional gender stereotypes. Thus we see him presenting the Prodigal Father (Lk 15) as someone in the traditionally female role of passively waiting for the son, and then acting as the traditional mother by responding with pity and kissing him. In the same chapter he uses the image of the woman searching for a lost coin, which was a sign of wealth and independence that might more commonly be associated with men.[1] He takes women seriously, responds to them, and is changed by his dialogue with them. An example is the Canaanite woman in Matthew 15 who challenges his exclusive view about the audience for whom the good news is intended. We see him also engaged in serious theological dialogue with the woman at the well in John 4 and with Martha in John 11. He broke social taboos in his relationships with women, by touching them, for example, Peter's mother-in-law (Lk 4) and Jairus's daughter (Lk 8) and allowing them to touch him (the sinful woman in Lk 7). He did not purify himself after being touched by the haemorrhaging woman (Lk 8). Women responded well to him. Not only were they the people who stood by his cross (although it should be remembered that it would have been more dangerous for the men to do so) but they were the first to believe in the resurrection. Typically their story of the empty tomb was at first dismissed (Lk 24).

In the early church women played a prominent role in the ministry. Lydia ran a house church in Philippi (Acts 16:14, 40). Priscilla, together with her husband Aquila, led house churches in Corinth, Ephesus and Rome (Rom 16:3-5). Phoebe, a deaconess, (Paul uses the same word for men as for women) travelled from church to church preaching the gospel (Rom 16:1).

All this suggests that Jesus was very different in his treatment of women and in his understanding of the feminine in God from what we have traditionally imagined. The same is true of at least part of the Hebrew scriptures and of the early church. We need to respond to this not simply by putting women into traditional ministries in our churches, but by changing radically the way that we relate to each other. Part of this involves putting a much greater stress on our relationships. Women tend to place greater emphasis than men on relationships, although this is slowly changing. In local communities it tends to be women, rather than men, who stress bread and butter issues rather than ideology. This is because they still have the traditional female role of motherhood.

Comment

Would a new emphasis in the church on the place and gifts of women make a difference to our situation in Northern Ireland? I think it might. It would certainly, as I have argued, help interchurch relationships if all Catholics presented more balanced notions of Mary's relationship to God and of her role as mediatrix and this in turn would help the context in which politics is done. Secondly, many women have discovered the feminine as well as the masculine in God, and the role of Mary as faith companion as well as mother. They know the deep need that both men and women have for reciprocal, respectful relationships. If such women occupied positions of power and influence in our church, then it would make a significant impact on our politics. They would be much more likely to be critical of both nationalism and unionism. They would have much less patience with political structures that excluded deprived people. They would be much more instinctive in calling for changes needed to enable women to take jobs more easily. Protestant and Catholic women, because of their common experience of oppression, would have an emotive vision to bond them, and one that might be strong enough to stand up to the pull of nationalism, be it of the Irish or British variety. There could be a potent new weapon for peace if women, especially those from deprived Catholic and Protestant areas, could unite together more often.

The issue, then, is not simply one of having more women in

positions of power and influence, because women are as likely as men to act in a destructive way. The task is rather one of giving scope to the talents and the leadership qualities of women who are committed to inclusive, respectful relationships.

JESUS AND THE OUTCASTS

The second group I want to look at in this section is people who are considered as outcasts by many in society. In his relationships with outcasts such as prostitutes, tax collectors, and foreigners, Jesus broke the social conventions of his day by eating with them. Again, for his Jewish audience this was a direct scandal. To eat with someone was to have a relationship with them. Those who were righteous, that is those who kept the myriad of Jewish laws, could not have a relationship with sinners, because that would make them unclean. The righteous could only have fellowship with others who were righteous. Jesus denied this by having table-fellowship with those who were officially sinners, and in some cases who were also unrepentant sinners.

Theologians speak of Jesus's attitude to the poor and outcasts as part of his concern for justice. This was not in itself new: it had been central in the teaching of the Hebrew scriptures. But Jesus made two important changes.

The first was to extend the covenant – the agreement – that God made with his people to every person and culture in the world, many of whom were outcasts for the Jewish people. The second was to reveal that God's plan went far beyond justice to include mercy. What is meant by justice and mercy will be teased out further in our sections on the Prodigal Father and on the cross.

Prostitutes

Prostitution was punishable by death under Mosaic law because it broke the law. But in the eyes of the law the women must have been having sex by themselves because it was they alone and not the men who got stoned! Yet Jesus said that the prostitutes would be part of God's community before the religious leaders. Further, he entered into relationship with some of these women before they had shown any sign of repentance, as we can see in the case of the woman taken in adultery in John 8.

The tax collectors

There was an obvious reason why tax collectors were excluded from Jewish society: they were a major element in the oppression of the people. They collected taxes for the Roman occupiers, and creamed off whatever they could over and beyond this for themselves. Not only were they breaking specific religious laws but, in terms of the Hebrew scriptures, they were placing themselves outside the covenant community. The prophets were quite clear on this: those who oppressed the poor, widows, and orphans could have no place in God's community. Yet Jesus called one of them – Matthew – to be an apostle and he then ate and drank with his friends, presumably before these had shown any inclination for conversion. He stayed with Zacchaeus – who was also a tax collector – and from the story it is suggested that Zacchaeus's decision to change his ways came after Jesus' decision to stay with him. Jesus also constantly told the Jewish religious leaders that the tax collectors would be part of God's community before them.

Foreigners

Jesus seemed to relate to foreigners, in some cases, in a way that deliberately antagonised the Jewish leaders. The story of the Good Samaritan (Lk 10) was simply a story or parable. Yet he decided to make the neighbour in his story of the injured man a Samaritan, precisely because the Samaritans were enemies of the Jews. Similarly he makes a point of commenting on the fact that out of the ten lepers who were healed the one who returned to give thanks was a Samaritan (Lk 17). The centurion who showed greater faith than Jesus had seen elsewhere, when he asked for his servant to be healed, was a Roman officer. This moved Jesus to remark that 'many will come from the east and the west' to sit at the heavenly banquet (Lk 7). Again this was an extension of Jewish notions of who would be present in the afterlife. Jesus says directly that belonging to the Chosen People as such will not be a means of salvation. Salvation now depends on relationships with other people and with God in this world.

The incident of the cure of the daughter of the Canaanite woman (Mt 15) is an example of Jesus being particularly impressed by a foreigner. At first he refused her request because he had been sent only to the people of Israel. There are no grounds for assuming that this is simply an example of Jesus testing the woman in order to draw greater faith out of her. His response was perfectly appropriate for a Jewish teacher of the time. But the woman challenged his position. When Jesus said, 'It's not right to take the children's food and throw it to the dogs', she replied 'But even the dogs eat the leftovers that fall from their masters' table!' There seems a note of surprise in Jesus' reply: 'You are a woman of great faith.'

What is being suggested here is that during his life Jesus as a human person grew in his understanding of his mission. At first he conceived of it as directed only to the people of Israel. Later he began to see the implications of the good news of salvation for the rest of the world.

It is worth noting that this journey, which Jesus seems to have gone through, is paralleled by the first major crisis the early Jewish Christians faced: namely, the place of the Gentiles in God's plan of salvation. One illustration of this is the story of Peter and Cornelius in Acts chapter 10. We are told that Peter had a dream one day while praying. In his dream he is hungry and a sheet is let down from heaven with all sort of animals in it. Peter is told to kill them and eat them. As a good Jew he cannot eat animals that the Jews regarded as unclean. So he refuses. Yet three times in the dream the blanket is let down from heaven with the same command.

At the same time as Peter was having his dream we are told that Cornelius, a Roman centurion, but 'a devout man who feared God with all his household, gave alms liberally to the people, and prayed constantly to God' (Acts 10:2), was also having a vision. In it he was told to send some men to Joppa and to ask Peter to visit him.

Peter learnt from his visit to Cornelius that 'God has shown me that I should not call any man or woman common or unclean' (Acts 10:28). He realised that 'God has no partiality, but in every nation any one who fears him and does what is right is acceptable to him' (10:34). The story ends with Cornelius and his household being given the gift of the Holy Spirit, even though they have not yet been baptised.

This story was part of the slow and painful journey in which the early Jewish followers of Jesus learnt that his message and his hope were not only for the Chosen People of the Hebrew scriptures, but for everyone. Another part of the same journey was the struggle by Paul, which was ultimately successful, to persuade the church that it was not necessary for Gentiles to be circumcised, or to follow Jewish dietary rules in order to be followers of Christ.

It needs to be remembered that the first covenant, between God and the Jewish people, was never revoked. It is still in place: God is still their God; they are still God's people. What has happened is that as a result of the gradual growth that took place in Our Lord's understanding, and of the journey of the early church with respect to the Gentiles, outsiders like ourselves have now been included in this covenant.

The fact that God's community is inclusive is of central importance. The Northern Ireland conflict is about exclusivity: British people excluding the Irish, nationalists excluding members of the security forces, the people of the Republic distancing themselves from the north, and Christians separating themselves from non-Christians, etc. What our analysis suggests is that in so far as we act in this way as a community, to that extent we separate ourselves from God's community.

This is not to suggest that we should never be involved in conflict, or that we should never confront people when they are wrong. But it tells us something about the way we should conduct our conflicts: by recognising our own temptation to self-righteousness, by seeing those we oppose and who harm us as still our brothers and sisters; and by working on our side of the relationship so that there is never any block to a full reconciliation coming from us.

2. GOD RECONCILES

Mercy and forgiveness
The second issue on which Jesus departed from – or perhaps developed – Hebrew scripture teaching was that of mercy. The standard teaching of Mosaic law was 'an eye for an eye and a tooth for a tooth.' The God presented in the Hebrew scriptures is often an angry God who punishes those who depart from the law, or oppress the poor, or oppose Israel, his Chosen People. But even in the Hebrew scriptures this picture is modified by the loving Father, who continually contradicts himself by failing to carry out his promises of wrath, and who ends up forgiving his people. The covenant is never broken on God's side, but only by the people, and it is the same covenant that is renewed.

However, Jesus introduced a radical change. 'You have heard that it was said, "An eye for an eye, and a tooth for a tooth." But now I tell you: do not take revenge on someone who wrongs you. If anyone slaps you on the right cheek, let him slap your left cheek too. And if someone takes you to court to sue you for your shirt, let him have your coat as well ...' (Mt 5). This, and similar passages, raise an issue which is absolutely central to the conflict in these islands: that of forgiveness.

Forgiveness was so important to Jesus that he told people first to be reconciled with their enemies, then to come and offer their gifts on the altar. Offering a gift to his Father at the same time as there was enmity between members of the community was to him a contradiction of the meaning of worship. One could not be in relationship with the Father without being in relationship with other people. This in itself was not new, in that in the Hebrew scriptures those who broke the covenant by abusing the poor thereby put themselves outside the community. But, as many commentators have pointed out, Jesus's teaching goes further. He not only insists that we should have nothing against our neighbour, but that our neighbour should have nothing against us. This can be interpreted in a fundamentalist way to suggest that we should hold no religious services while there is any form of conflict. It might be no harm if we tended in that direction in Britain and in Ireland, north and south, because as things stand, we exaggerate in the opposite direction. But, presumably, Jesus means a situation where our neighbour holds something against us with good reason, and something for which we are responsible.

We should not assume that forgiveness was easy for Jesus. His anger at various times was deep and his words extreme. We have perhaps tended to forget this, both because anger is often seen – quite wrongly – as something that religious people should not experience, and secondly because we have become so familiar with his words that they have lost their sting. You would perhaps be annoyed if you were described in tones of ringing condemnation as 'a stinking, rotten, heap of flesh'. Yet that would be mild compared with the words Jesus used to describe the Pharisees: 'You are like whitewashed tombs, which look fine on the outside but are full of bones and decaying corpses on the inside' (Mt 23:27). As always, we need to distinguish between what the early church attributed to Jesus and what he actually said. But there are enough instances of Jesus speaking like this scattered throughout the gospels, together with the incident of the cleansing of the Temple, to suggest that Jesus was not blessed with a placid, gentle temperament that could never be roused to fury.

Yet the same person who felt this fury at what the religious leaders of his time were doing to people, faced rejection, a mock trial and death, without responding with anger. Further, he not only forgave them for what they did, he pleaded on their behalf with the Father. One could almost say that he told lies on their behalf by saying 'They know not what they do', because on different occasions he had confronted them by saying their hardness of heart was all the worse because they *did* know what they were doing. In fact both interpretations are possible. Within the context of his dialogue with the Father, the Pharisees did not know what they were doing, because they had not yet experienced being caught up in the love of that relationship in the way Jesus had. Within human terms, and within the context of Hebrew scriptural teaching about the coming of the Messiah, the scribes and Pharisees had sufficient knowledge to accept Jesus as Messiah. Yet they refused to do so.

Did Jesus forgive his enemies before they had repented? The answer is clearly yes, but we need to sort out what we mean by forgiveness. In the case of Matthew's tax collector friends with whom he shared a meal (Mt 9), of Zacchaeus in whose house he chose to stay (Lk 19), of the paralytic whose sins were forgiven even though he himself had given no sign of repentance (it was his friends who had carried him to Jesus) (Lk 5), of the woman who was taken in adultery (Jn 8), in all these cases Jesus enters into a relationship with sinners and in some cases forgives their sins, before we are told anything about their repentance. Similarly, on the cross, the plea for forgiveness is uttered while the scribes and Pharisees have clearly not repented (Lk 23).

Does this mean that Jesus' forgiveness restores the relationship with the sinner without any response on their part? Clearly not. What it shows is that Jesus will not give up on anyone, that from his side the relationship will never end, that he will continue to seek out sinners. Further, as in the case of Zacchaeus, Jesus's choice of the sinner may lead to a speedy conversion. It was after Jesus had chosen to stay in his house that Zacchaeus said he would repay all he owed.

This shows that in Jesus we are given a picture of a God who is desperately and painfully anxious to mend broken relationships. This cannot and will not be done by pretending that sin is unimportant, or that people can oppress the poor. Such behaviour provokes deep fury in God. But that anger will never block the need that God has for the relationship between himself and his people to be restored. The anger comes from the pain that the broken relationship causes God.

The Parable of the Prodigal Father
One of the great stories that Jesus told when teaching people about God was that of the Prodigal Father. It is one of the times in the bible when God is presented as a bad listener. If you read the story (Lk 15) notice the speech the son made up when he came to his senses. It is quite long as a gospel speech and it makes assumptions about the kind of relationship that it will be possible for him to have with his father in future: that of a servant. What happens when he

meets the father is that his speech is cut short and the content of it is completely ignored by the father. The father's immediate response is to kiss his son, to order a feast to be held for him and to seat him at the place of honour. Before this, of course, the kind of person the father is has been shown by the fact that he recognised the son from afar off. This could only have happened if he had been looking out for him and doing so all the hours of every day. Otherwise he would not have seen him until he arrived at the house. His verbal response is not to his son at all: it is to his servants, ordering the feast to be prepared. His only direct response to his son is non-verbal: he kisses and hugs him, and puts him in the place of honour at the feast.

Many commentators have drawn attention to the moment in the story where we are told the son came to his senses, and began to remember his father's house. But the second change the son went through is at least as significant as the first. When he started out on the journey to his father he has no doubt that he has done wrong, but when he meets his father he is asked to accept a change of status: to move from the servant status that he had hoped to be given by the father, to that of the principal guest sitting at the father's right hand at the feast held to honour him. In the story the son accepted that change. 'Why not?', we may well ask. In fact one of the most difficult moments in the restoration of a relationship is where the person or community who has done wrong overcomes their shame and accepts themselves as the other partner sees them. The story is often rightly called the story of the Prodigal Father, because the amazing love of the father is the main focus. But the younger son, the sinner, who accepts his new status of honour, also plays an important role in it.

But what of the older son, who had always remained faithful to the father, who had worked for him year in and year out, and who had never had as much as a goat with which to celebrate with his friends? His focus has been wrong. It has been placed on himself, in isolation from his father and from the family. He has not been deeply concerned about the loss of his brother. He has not felt compassion for his brother who was lost. He has never actually been part of the community, despite his good works. In his self-righteousness he has placed himself where he is shown in the story – outside the feast, and so outside the community.

Forgiveness is perhaps the most difficult of the demands Our Lord makes in the gospels. But there is no mistaking the fact that his followers are asked to take it on. So central was it to his teaching that it is included in the 'Our Father', the central prayer of all Christians: 'Forgive us our trespasses as we forgive those who trespass against us.' Only to the extent that we forgive others, do we ask God to forgive us. There is no more difficult prayer in Christendom. It does not mean that we avoid anger. We saw above how often Jesus showed anger in the gospels. Nor does it mean that we pretend injustices do not exist.

Does this mean that we let people get away with terrible injustices? In a sense the answer is 'Yes': we may have to let people get away with things. Or rather, we may have to accept that they appear to do so. But this does not mean that in fact injustice goes unnoticed by God, or that when we commit injustice we will not ultimately have to face the people that we have wronged. What it does mean is that when we suffer injustice ourselves we have to let go of our bitterness, as distinct from our anger. We have to give up notions of revenge. We need also to be careful about looking for punishment for those who have offended us: it is almost impossible for us to do this without in some way looking for revenge.

For people who have been bereaved in the 'Troubles' in Northern Ireland talk of forgiveness is particularly difficult. Gordon Wilson, whose daughter was murdered in the Enniskillen bomb on Remembrance Sunday in 1987, is an example of someone who was able to forgive her killers immediately afterwards. Not many are able to do this. Nor does following Christ necessarily require us to forgive immediately. Christians are asked to forgive as humans, albeit humans with a special grace. For us, forgiveness is often a slow and dark process that at times seems completely impossible.[2] Many will not be able to pray the 'Our Father' without changing the words to something like: 'Forgive us our trespasses, not as we forgive others, but as we would like to be able to forgive others, that is, in the way you forgive them.' The normal process of grieving takes time, and it involves different stages of denial, anger, bargaining and slow acceptance. Nor do these stages follow one another in a straight linear fashion. In the end, however, we are asked by God to forgive. However difficult this task is, and however long it takes us, we cannot get away from the fact that this is what God asks of us. To stay in bitterness is to stay in a prison. This is one of the terrible ironies of unjust suffering: victims experience injustice in the first place, but if they cannot eventually respond with forgiveness they are to an extent destroyed as human beings. They separate themselves from God until they can forgive.

Is the same thing also asked of us as communities? The answer again is 'Yes' and it is equally difficult. The historical and current hurts that Irish people have experienced from British and unionist people need to be forgiven, even before any proper repentance is made for these crimes. The same demand is made of British people to forgive the hurts imposed on them by those of us who are Irish.

Notes:
1 Claire Colette Murphy, SHCJ, *An introduction to Christian Feminism*, Dublin: Dominican Publications, 1994.
2 *Burying our dead: political funerals in NI*, Belfast: An Interchurch Group on Faith and Politics, 1992.

CHAPTER 5

The Son who faces conflict and the cross

1. THE GOD OF CONFLICT

The temptations

Many Christians ignore the degree of conflict that there was in the life of Jesus. So often Christianity presents a bland picture of him. To some extent this is due to our natural desire to avoid conflict. But it also means that we often fail as groups to deal properly with anger. If we fail to deal with anger it does not go away. It remains in us and eats away at our energy and our life. Ultimately it causes depression. Reconciliation can often be used as a means of avoiding conflict. Statements like, 'We are all one in Christ', 'We all worship the one God', while having a grain of truth, can also be a mechanism to avoid the truth of our divisions. That is one of the reasons why reconciliation must always be linked with justice.

Even a cursory reading of the gospels shows an immense amount of conflict in Jesus's public life. But this conflict was not simply between Jesus and external parties. It was also within himself. The gospels present this internal conflict in the life of Jesus as temptations.

The temptations must have been an embarrassing aspect of his life for the gospel writers. Yet, because they are mentioned in all three of the synoptic gospels, we can be reasonably certain that Jesus went through some period of significant disturbance. In fact it is not unreasonable to assume that Our Lord had a series of temptations for much of his life, and that the gospel writers presented these as taking place in the single incident of the temptations in the desert. This is a reasonable deduction because there are clear symbolic elements in the gospel accounts. The forty days of Jesus's fast is an obvious parallel with the forty years the Chosen People spent in the desert after they were freed from Egypt and before they were given the law on Mount Sinai.

Also, the references to temptations are not confined to this story. A second is the time when he asked 'Who do men say that I am?'

(Mt 16:13). Immediately after this incident Matthew tells of the incident where Jesus speaks of his suffering and death, although Luke edits this out of his account (Lk 9). Peter responds by saying that this must never happen. Jesus's response is vehement: 'Get behind me Satan!' The vehemence suggests that as the popularity of his mission was fading Jesus was facing the prospect of deepening conflict, including the possibility of his death, and was struggling to accept this.

Thirdly, the agony in the garden is a clear example of Jesus breaking down in fear and anguish at the prospect that faced him. It was a cry of despair to his Father to find some other way of fulfilling the mission which had come from the Father but which the Son had embraced.

Finally, on the cross, the cry of abandonment 'My God, my God why have you forsaken me?' has been variously interpreted as Jesus saying Psalm 22 and as an experience of being forsaken by God.

What were the temptations about? In both Matthew and Luke they are about the same three things: turning bread into stones, gaining possession of all the kingdoms of the world in return for worshipping Satan, and throwing himself off the mount of the temple to see if God will save him.

The fast solution

The most obvious explanation of the first temptation – to turn stones into bread – is that Jesus was tempted throughout his life to solve poverty and pain by miracles, by literally turning the stones into bread so that people who were at starvation level would be fed. The temptation came from the compassion he felt for people who were suffering, and from his fierce anger at this. The easy and quick answer was a miracle. That was not the answer his Father wanted. It was not an answer that would have taken us seriously as free human beings. In the end, because he resisted the temptation, we know that it was not the answer that Jesus himself wanted.

Usually there are no fast solutions to conflicts. There is no replacement for the slow growth of trust between separated communities, and for the hard work needed to develop new and more respectful political structures.

The temptation to be a political messiah

The resistance to the temptation to become a wonder-worker is paralleled by the second temptation: to become a political messiah. Jesus certainly had contact with the Zealots. We know this because

Simon, one of the Apostles, had been one of them. For anyone interested in reforming society in Palestine, joining the Zealots was one
of several options. They were dedicated to freeing the land from the
Romans, so that the worship of God could take place in a Jerusalem
free from domination by foreigners and pagans. This would free the
people both religiously and politically. It would also break the burden of taxes demanded by the Romans. The Zealots used violence
in the failed uprising against the Romans in 66AD. Parallels can
easily be drawn between them and modern day paramilitaries,
although the religious framework of the Zealots would clearly have
been different.

Some theologians suggest that Jesus himself may have been
attracted to leading a violent revolution against the Romans. One
pointer is the story of the feeding of the 5000 (Jn 6). This is usually
presented as a prefiguring of the eucharist, or as a symbol of the
richness of the word of God. Undoubtedly the miracle would have
reminded Jesus's Jewish audience of God feeding the people with
manna in the desert (Exod 16). But the political implications of the
story also need to be stressed. Albert Nolan argues that the incident
was an attempt by a large group of people to persuade Jesus to
become a political messiah. However, Jesus wanted to achieve something much more radical: a new relationship between all peoples.[1]

John alone adds the detail that after the miracle of sharing Jesus
could see that they wanted to make him king. But both Mark and
Matthew say Jesus made the disciples get into a boat and that he
sent the crowd away. This suggests that the crowd did not willingly
disperse. All four gospels see Jesus spending a long time in prayer
after the miracle (John implies this rather than stating it directly)
and they all place the incident of walking on the water after this
prayer. Why this sequence? It suggests that this was a very significant moment in Jesus' life, that he made a crucial decision at this
time, that this was in some way associated deeply with his
Father/Mother, with whom he spent the night in prayer, that it was
also associated with tribulation for the disciples – the storm at sea –
and with his own transcendence which the post-resurrection
church emphasised.

At the very least the incident suggests that Jesus thought deeply
about political, social and economic oppression and about ways to
change them.

The second incident that shows Jesus thought deeply about
these issues is the clearing of the temple. It was not a spontaneous
reaction of anger by Jesus. He came to the Temple the evening

before, but since it was too late to do anything he went away and came back the following day (Mk 11:11). Obviously he brought a large group of followers with him, otherwise the traders would never have let him interfere with them as they did.

This incident may have been the immediate cause of the shift from an enthusiastic response from the people to Jesus' public teaching to a situation where he withdrew with his disciples and went on the run. He could not appear in Jerusalem, except with large crowds; he even had to withdraw from Galilee to the region of Tyre and Sidon.

This shift in the ministry towards a situation of conflict is marked by all the gospels. Jesus certainly became well known as a troublemaker to the Jewish authorities, and probably also to the Romans.

During this period Jesus also seems to have been tempted to use violence at least for the protection of himself and his followers. To his disciples he said, 'But now if you have a purse, take it; if you have a haversack, do the same; if you have no sword, sell your cloak and buy one' (Lk 22:35-36).

In the end, however, Jesus refused to accept the role of a political messiah. The change that he was seeking involved not only a change of ruler – as a religious Jew he would almost certainly have wanted Jerusalem to be in the hands of Jewish rulers – but also a change in the nature of authority. His disciples must not lord it over people like the Gentiles do. 'For the Son of Man also came not to be served but to serve, and to give his life as a ransom for many' (Mk 10:45).

This is not to suggest that there were no political implications of Jesus's work. The new relationships that he was working for would certainly have undermined Roman rule, had he been successful, because their rule was based on fear and oppression. They would have destroyed the basis of Pharisaical rule, based as it was on a law that dominated men and women rather than being their servant. These relationships would also have undermined the basis of economic oppression by changing the way that tax collectors did business, as was shown by Zacchaeus when he responded to Jesus. Jesus's whole public life was aimed at the way people related to each other, and therefore involved political processes. Everything he said about service as opposed to domination was in practice a challenge to the way the Romans controlled Palestine, as well as confronting the scribes and the Pharisees. He was concerned with a change that would be deeper than that brought about simply by changing the political rulers.

A reading of the gospels, then, does not absolve us from the effort to change political structures to make them more just, more inclusive, and more participative. But it should also alert us to the limits of political structural change on its own. It is part of the equation and an important part of it. One has only to look at how the creation of the EU has changed the lives of millions for better or worse and the impact it has had on culture and values to recognise this point. But in turn values and culture have a profound impact on political structures and their stability or lack of it. The history of Eastern Europe where nationalism re-emerged once communism collapsed is witness to this.

Jesus was clear that new relationships could not be forced on men and women through violence because to do so would deny them the freedom and responsibility of choice. At the very least this should bias the Christian towards the rejection of violence. It was not Our Lord's way in a context of injustice, division, and occupation. Why, then, should it be ours? However, to say this does not absolve the Christian from involvement in non-violent conflicts. The idea that Christianity is a soft religion, or that it does not involve confronting injustices in society, simply does not stand up to even a cursory reading of the gospels. The way of peace, for the Christian, is not about the avoidance of conflict, but rather about finding creative ways to engage in constructive relationships that will certainly involve conflict, but which will not fill the graveyards with the bodies of victims, each of which, at one level, symbolises a defeat for God's community. Such a stance is paralleled by some non-Christians. Gandhi stressed the active component in non-violence. But he always looked as well for some surprising and symbolic action which would introduce a new element into the conflict and which would allow for the possibility of new thinking and new relationships to emerge.

Many commentators have pointed out the active non-violence strategy that was used in many of Jesus's best known sayings, which have often been taken out of context to mean supine passivism. For example the injunction to give one's shirt when one's cloak was demanded was a means of outflanking the persecutor. The context was someone insisting on repayment of debt which a poor person could not do. If the creditor brought the debtor to court and insisted on taking the outer garment, Jesus's advice is to give the undergarment as well. The result is that the person is left naked. Nakedness was taboo in Judaism but the person blamed for it was the person who caused it. So the tables are turned on the creditor. This is an example of Jesus accepting the reality of the weakness of the poor in his society but also thinking out non-violent strategies that they could use to get a measure of justice.[2]

It is worthwhile for Catholics to ask what the major temptations are that we face as a community. To answer 'none' is simply to display ignorance. The most obvious temptations have been to ignore the conflict, the option chosen by so many both north and south, and secondly to engage in violence, the option chosen by a small number, with disastrous consequences. Each temptation springs from a deeper lack within us as a community: the lack of a spirituality that would enable us to engage the world in which we live. By this I mean that we are still burdened with a spirituality that is both other-worldly and individualistic. A startling example of this is the experience of a friend of mine who went to Mass in Belfast the day after the IRA ceasefire was announced in 1994: there was no mention of the ceasefire during the Mass. I cannot say how widespread such an attitude is. But the impression given very often by many Catholic parishes during the period of violence was that there was nothing they could do about it: their task was a spiritual one, and so did not involve 'politics'.

The self-righteous

Many of Christ's conflicts were with the self-righteous, especially the Pharisees, and not with 'sinners'. Why was he so hard on the Pharisees? After all they were trying to live good lives, according to their lights. They kept the Mosaic law. They went to the synagogue. They gave tithes. They said their prayers. What more could they do? Further, they were not like tax collectors, who not only collaborated with the Romans in oppressing the people, but also broke the Mosaic law in doing so.

A possible answer is that Jesus thought that the Jewish people suffered far more oppression from the Pharisees than they did from the Romans. It was not that Jesus was pro-Roman. He was not. He condemned the way they lorded it over their subjects, but he realised that the Pharisees were capable of oppressing the people at a deeper level, because it was oppression from within. The Romans imposed harsh laws on the people and they denied them freedom. But they did not convince them that they were sinners, that they were worse than other people. It was the Pharisees who took on that task. They made the laws that determined whether a person was good or evil. They ensured that there were such a myriad of laws that only the educated could know them and therefore have the possibility of fulfilling them. They saw themselves as better than others, and expected others to do the same. They had no compassion for their fellow human beings. That was why Jesus was so angry with them.

An example is the story of the Pharisee and the Publican (Lk 18). The Pharisee not only keeps the law but is grateful to God for his ability to do so. The tax collector asks for mercy as a sinner, but we are not told of any purpose of amendment on his part. But the difference between the two men is that the Pharisee – like the elder son in the story of the Prodigal – thought that he was better than the tax collector. The tax collector had no such illusions in regard to the Pharisee. In Jesus' eyes that is why the tax collector was right with God and the Pharisee was not.[3]

The conflict in Jesus's life is a sign of the conflict that should be expected among his followers: if there is no conflict perhaps we should ask ourselves if we are preaching or living the gospel at all. At the same time we need to be aware of self-righteousness: there is almost certainly some wrong on our side as well as on our opponents.

Comment

The temptations of Jesus are particularly relevant to Christians in Northern Ireland. We need to avoid the temptation to flee to prayer as an escape from tough questions that need to be raised. Prayers for peace can sometimes be like this. It is not the prayers that are wrong, but that so often we are waiting for a miracle to happen – to other people: that they will change and become less bigoted. Whereas what our prayer should do is impel us to action to change what lies within our power to change. Perhaps we need less pilgrimages and more prayerful seminars on what our stance as Christians should be on issues like Articles Two and Three of the Constitution of the Republic, or the changes required to make policing more acceptable to northern nationalists, to take some examples.

Secondly, we need to reflect on our Lord's temptation to become a political messiah. Churches err on the side of non-involvement in politics. They often claim to preach a 'spiritual' gospel in which politics has no place. That is not the way that Jesus lived. He was deeply aware that his words and actions were filled with political implications. Certainly, clergy need to avoid the temptation to become politicians in the party sense. We should also respect the proper autonomy of politicians. But it is especially appropriate for the church, both clerical and lay, to be involved in a critique of the values that lie behind our political systems.

Churches as a whole need to develop greater respect for the noble art of politics. It is politicians who have to make tough decisions, often with very deep consequences. Many people in Northern Ireland have been deeply critical of them and have scapegoated them for the whole conflict. But these people were shouting from the sidelines, they themselves were not involved in politics. It was beneath them. That is not the sort of stance encouraged by looking at the story of Jesus and the temptations. His response was to get involved.

Thirdly, the temptation most of us face is to ignore the conflict, to pretend that everything is all right, that we would have 'a grand wee country' here if only the men and women of violence would stop. Now that they have stopped, are all our problems solved? By no means.

Fourthly, we can be tempted by impatience, the need for a fast solution. Violence is a temptation of that kind. So is a failure to take account of the deep and understandable pain that so many groups feel. This drives them towards conflict, of either a violent or non-violent nature. It makes both reconciliation and justice difficult because people can respond with defensiveness. In the face of this it is easy to be tempted by despair.

Fifthly, we need to be at least as aware of oppression that is imposed from within our community as from without. This is especially important in considering the place of women within the church. The deepest oppression felt by many Catholic women who are committed to the church is that which they experience from the church itself, not from society. So also in Northern Ireland we need to look at agencies that oppress Catholics not only from outside but also from within the community.

Sixthly, Jesus's attitude to the self-righteous challenges all our tendencies to scapegoat other groups. Thus if we see ourselves as the only recipients of God's grace we are likely to be putting ourselves outside God's community. This does not mean that we have to be complete relativists. Paramilitary activity and illegal killings by the state, for example, are wrong. But we need to be careful to ask ourselves how we were involved in the series of relationships that led to violence, rather than simply condemning those involved in it. The conflict is taking place in these islands. There must therefore be some factors in our history, or religion, or economics, or our other relationships that make it easier for the conflict to take place here than in other places.

The image of God that Jesus reveals is of a God who engages in conflict where necessary, and there is always need for it in any society, because there is always a need to oppose oppression. However, for the Christian, the life of Christ gives certain guidelines for the way we take part in conflict: one is to avoid violence almost always; a second is to look for strategies that will threaten and undermine the power of those who oppress people; a third is to struggle with love for those who commit oppression, as well as for their victims; a fourth is to recognise that peacemaking often involves deep searching to find out what is the right path to take. Finally we need to be aware of self-righteousness, and that, while failure is certainly part of what following Christ entails, often our failures are self-induced. Humility, then, and an openness to the strategies of others are in order.

2. THE GOD WHO SUFFERS

Jesus, the cross and failure

One of the scandals the early church had to struggle with was that Jesus failed in his mission – as they saw it – initially. The climax of this failure came on the cross: he trusted in his divine Father to save him, to bring about somehow the success of his mission. But the only response he got from the Father was silence.

This is the relevance of the third temptation: to throw himself off the top of the temple in Jerusalem and to see if God will save him. At some stage in the middle of his ministry Jesus knew that the people were turning against him and that the leaders of the people were going to oppose him, even to the extent of killing him. How could this be possible if he were God's Son? How could his mission fail? He must have been tempted not to trust his Father to the death. He must have thought of somehow forcing the Father's hand. If God intervened directly, then perhaps a different way of completing the mission could be found.

But God did not intervene. The Father did not protect him. He did not save him from the consequences of giving us freedom. The temptation to try and force God to intervene directly comes up a second time in the agony in the garden: 'If you will, take this cup of suffering away from me. Not my will, however, but your will be done' (Lk 22:42 Good News). But when this temptation passed Jesus went to the darkness of his death, to his rejection by the leaders of the people and by the crowd, to his betrayal by Judas, and to the fleeing of his closest followers. On the cross the expectant crowd waited to see if Elijah would come to save him (Mt 27:49), but neither Elijah nor the Father came. Jesus had entered into our world and he faced the consequences of becoming one of us to the full. By all human criteria – except those of faithfulness and courage – his life ended in failure and destruction. 'Jesus died without a word or a wink from God to reassure him that, whatever the gawking crowd might think, he knew that Jesus was not only innocent but valid where it mattered.'[4]

A proper understanding of the meaning of the cross is crucial to our notion of God, because it has been used in the past to support the notion of a God who is outside the world, who is beyond suffering, and also to idealise suffering in this world as somehow a good thing in itself.

Some theologians argue that the meaning of the cross can only be found in the relationship of the three Persons to each other.[5] Here it seems particularly appropriate to think of the First Person at times as Father and at other times as Mother, because each description opens up another aspect, however small, of the divine mystery. Paul tells us that God did not spare his own Son but gave him up for all of us (Rom 8:32). He sees the cry on the cross 'My God, my God, why have you forsaken me?' (Mt 27:46) as an anguished experience of abandonment by God. Other commentators disagree and see the saying as the start of Psalm 22, which ends up as a prayer of hope and trust. However, the theme of the Father handing over the Son (*paradidonai* in the Greek) is developed in other parts of the New Testament (Rom 8:32, Gal 2:20). Moltmann sees the cross as a double forsakenness: the Son is abandoned by the Father, and the Father who hands him over suffers the death of the Son. As O'Donnell puts it, 'In this moment of the cross, the divine being is rent asunder. Father and Son are held apart by death, darkness and sin'.[6] Thus both the Father and the Son suffer at the cross. This thesis challenges the traditional notion of a God who is above suffering because he is unchangeable.

The suggestion that God the Mother suffers at the cross intimates that, like the Son, she did not want the cross. (In this section when I refer to the Mother at the cross I am referring to God the Mother and not to Mary the mother of Jesus.) She wanted Christ's mission to be successful. She wanted the people to be converted, to accept Christ as the Son of God, to change their relationships with each other, to end their oppression, to give up telling lies in court, and violence, and denying people their rights as human beings. In short the Mother, like the Son, wanted people to love each other both individually and socially. The failure of this project meant the death of the Son. As human beings, those of us who have not lost a child can only imagine such a pain. But the pain of the Mother was greater than this, because not only was her love for Jesus obviously greater than any human love, but she also lost – at least temporarily – the people who rejected Christ. The message of Christ was that these too were God's sons and daughters, adopted as such in Christ. God's pain, then, was not only over the loss of Christ, but over the loss of all her children.

For the Son, part of the destruction of the cross involved him becoming sin. Paul writes: 'God made him who knew no sin to be sin so that we might become the righteousness of God' (2 Cor 5:21). The Son on the cross is identified with our sin. A definition of sin is that it is separating ourselves from God, as well as separating ourselves from each other. Hell then is eternal separation from God and from others. The cry of forsakenness on the cross can be seen as a cry of the Son experiencing the despair of being separated from the Mother. Becoming sin he experienced the total loneliness and emptiness of separation. An analogy for us is to look at the effect our own sins have had on us: the way we have been separated from others and from God by the wrong we have done. In Christ's case, because he experienced his love for his Mother in a way that we have not, and because becoming sin involved in some sense entering into the worst of human hatred, the pain involved is incalculably greater.

But what was the purpose of this abandonment into which the three Persons together willingly entered? How was this meant to solve the problem of our sinfulness? Hans Urs von Balthasar gives some clue to this mystery in his meditation on Holy Saturday. He takes seriously the image of Christ descending into hell as a symbol of the Son entering into solidarity with those who have rejected God. He is going to stand beside them.[7]

In what way does this change the sinners? It leaves them their freedom to reject God. They remain autonomous human beings. They have chosen freely to be alone, to separate themselves from God and from God's community. But what God, through the action of Christ, is saying is that she will not leave them alone. The loving Mother will go after her children wherever they are and stand with them in their aloneness, waiting for them to turn from their chosen isolation to open themselves to God's eternal love. They will still be alone, by their own choice, but, paradoxically, they will be alone in the presence of Christ, sent by God.

In a sense the aloneness of the sinner will be something like the aloneness of Christ on the cross. The Mother seems completely absent. The Son experiences complete God-forsakenness. But of course the Mother cannot actually be absent. If we, for the most part, cannot abandon our children, neither can the Mother abandon her Son. But because the Son has been sent to seek out those who have separated themselves from God, God's presence is experienced by the Son as absence. In a similar way the sinner, who has chosen to separate himself or herself from Christ, will experience God and Christ as being absent. The reality is that both will be present and will continue to be present for all time.

The cross is a much more radical image of the forgiveness of God than the story of the prodigal father. There the father let the son go. That also happens with God and the sinner. But on the cross the crucial difference is revealed: in the story of the prodigal the father stays at home – even though he watches out for the son every day so that he is able to see him from a long way off. On the cross, however, the Mother sends her own Son into the far country, to stand alongside the sinner in his destructiveness. The cross is telling us that there are simply no limits to which God will not go in order to bring us to love each other freely.

Comment

For many people this is not good news. They have it firmly in their minds that the vast majority of people have not experienced Jesus Christ and because of this they are condemned to hell for all eternity. In this view the aim of God – who sent his Son into the world, not to condemn it, but so that the world might be saved through him (Jn 3:17) – that aim is frustrated and frustrated constantly. Not only did the mission of Christ fail during his own life, but it has been failing ever since.

How we interpret the cross is crucial for the way we live as Christians in Northern Ireland. If we see the Son's the descent into hell after his death as in some sense an image of God's ultimate refusal to let any of us go, as an image of the deep need that God has for us, then our attitude to the social aspect of faith will be very different. We will see other people either as part of God's community, or outside it. Clearly people place themselves out of relationship with God and are free to do so. But what matters is our attitude to them. We can hope that they will repent, turn away from their sins and come back to the community. But if they die in that state, for instance as paramilitaries, what is our attitude? Do we see them as having finally chosen to isolate themselves from God and therefore having no part in our concern? How far are we willing to go to be with people who have offended us? Are we willing to stand alongside them, as Christ was? Are we willing to experience forsakenness, as Christ did on the cross, because of our love for our enemies?

Notes:

1 Albert Nolan, *Jesus before Christianity*, London: DLT, 1977.

2 *cf* Walter Wink, 'Neither passivity nor violence: Jesus' third way, Mt 5:38-42 par.', in Willard Swartley, Editor, *The love of enemy and non-retaliation in the New Testament*, Westminster: John Knox Press, 1992.

3 Recently, there have been attempts to rehabilitate the Pharisees. *cf* William M. Thompson, *The Jesus Debate: a survey and synthesis*, NY: Paulist, 1985.

4 Leander Keck, *A future for the historical Jesus*, Nashville: Abingdon Press, 1971, p 229.

5 John J. O'Donnell, *The Mystery of the Triune God*, London: Sheed & Ward, 1987.

6 *ibid*, p 63.

7 Hans Urs von Balthasar, *Mysterium Paschale, The Mystery of Easter*, Edinburgh: T & T Clark, 1990.

CHAPTER 6

God triumphs

With all the pain and failure that there was in Christ's life, nonetheless Christians believe that his mission was a success: his community has already been established. One part of this confidence rests on the belief in the resurrection. The immediate reaction of the disciples to the crucifixion was despair. As the two men on the road to Emmaus put it: 'We had hoped that he was the Messiah ...'(Lk 24:21). However, it was not the end of the story. They went through an experience which led them to believe that Christ was alive and present to them. When they reflected and prayed about this afterwards, they remembered the promise that the Lord had made to send the Holy Spirit, who would be his Spirit, his presence in the world.

The reaction of the early disciples to this message was one of intense joy and this is reflected in the early chapters of the Acts of the Apostles. This joy was the basis of their forming a new community and sharing all things in common.

So central is the resurrection to the Christian story that we forget that for the early church it was the formative event, along with the coming of the Holy Spirit at Pentecost.

The resurrection was the first thing they preached about. Only later did they think of writing about Christ's historical life. In fact it is fair to say the gospels are really a narrative of the passion, death and resurrection of Christ, with an introduction relating to his historical life. That is why St Paul's writings, many of which pre-date the gospels, have so little on the historical Jesus.

To speak of God's kingdom, or community, makes no sense without the resurrection of Christ. It is obvious that justice and reconciliation will never be complete in this world, and that many millions will continue to die without being able to live in a context proper for human beings. The resurrection is the promise for them that something different is possible and that they will be brought into a world where their humanity can flourish.

There is a danger, of course, of using the resurrection in an escapist way and one that encourages us fatalistically to accept the sufferings of this world. That would be wrong. Rather the Christian message calls us to see it as a reality that is already present, although we cannot see it fully. We are called to live as people who are already risen, who have already entered into the new community that God has prepared for those who love her. To be part of God's community in the future we must live as part of it now. This is in part what St Paul is speaking about when he tells us that 'we have taken off the old self with its habits and put on the new self' (Col 3:9-10).

The joy of the resurrection can be seen today in many Christians in Northern Ireland who have come to believe in Christ and who work for the fulfilment of his community. Many of these are involved in the various communities who work for reconciliation and justice, some of which I listed in the introduction. Many of those who have been bereaved have also responded with a forgiveness and lack of bitterness that can only make sense in the context of the risen Christ. For example, some of the relatives of the UVF shooting in Loughinisland in June 1994, during the Republic of Ireland's world cup soccer match against Italy, were able to welcome the loyalist ceasefire the following October, and said they held no bitterness.

Part of what the resurrection means is that even in the face of the depth of evil that has been experienced in the Northern Ireland conflict, the risen Christ is at work in the situation. Within the context of God's plan for the world, he is drawing us into a community that can overcome the evil.

Universal salvation

One of the implications of the story of Jesus, especially if we follow Paul in seeing him identified with sin, is that God will never give up on any individual. Does this mean that all will be saved? There are plenty of texts in both the Hebrew scriptures and the New Testament to suggest the opposite. But to what extent are these texts threats comparable to the warnings that parents vehemently and with total seriousness issue to their children, but which in practice they never either mean or carry out? How much are they also a statement of the reality into which people put themselves by breaking their relationship with God and with other people? How much are they stating simply as a matter of fact that 'If you hate people who challenge injustice and do not speak the whole truth in court; if you oppress the poor and rob them of their grain' (Amos 5:10-11), then you will separate yourself from God and from other people? You will put yourself outside God's community.

What, then, about the gospel sayings about separation from God being eternal? Can these also be seen as threats, as warnings of the actual consequences of sin, as saying that as long as sinners maintain their sinful position, for so long they will be out of communion with God?

Clearly people will have different interpretations of these texts. However, the idea that God can leave people in hell and somehow forget them seems to reduce God to a moral level considerably below that attained by most human beings. The instances of humans – particularly women – abandoning their children are very rare. Such behaviour goes against our nature. It is considered crazy. Does this mean that the God who created us has not attained our moral stature? The alternative to this view seems to be accepting the possibility of universal salvation.

God's grace is offered to us freely and without merit on our part. But without our response, which must include our reconciliation with others where this is required, we cannot be reconciled to God, even though God's love for us and forgiveness of us still stands.

God cannot impose salvation on us against our will. In the end if one accepts the possibility of all being saved it will be a deduction based on the kind of person that Jesus was, on his compassion, on Jesus's own sayings about forgiveness, on a view of the cross as an act by God of profound solidarity with those who have rejected him, and on God's capacity to freely empower our conversion.

The hope of universal salvation is often pointed to as a teaching of an 'easy' God, one to whom sin does not matter. It is quite the opposite: the anger of Jesus and the destruction of the Son of God on the cross both point to the enormity of sin. But, enormous as sin is, God's love, God's generosity, and God's forgiveness, in the end, are greater.

If one accepts both the possibility of universal salvation and the depth of destruction caused by sin and oppression, this has implications for one's notion of what happens in the afterlife. If Jesus's work is ultimately to be successful then all men and women have to enter into community with each other. In the end there can be no outsiders. This suggests that all of us may have some peculiar neighbours in the next life. Would you enjoy the prospect of sharing heaven with your enemies? With Ian Paisley, or Gerry Adams, or Margaret Thatcher, or Charlie Haughey? Or even Adolf Hitler? Yet what kind of community will it be if any one of these is left out? How will God be able to tolerate the absence of one of her children, children she loves so much that she gave up her only begotten Son?

If God cannot give them up, how then can they enter her community? In the same way as the rest of us: by coming to terms with the ways they have harmed others, or failed to act in solidarity with those who suffered. By accepting the enormity of the harm they have done; by seeking forgiveness; by accepting the forgiveness, not only of the three Persons, but also of those they have harmed; and by offering forgiveness for the ways in which they have been oppressed. All this involves great suffering. In the light of the gospels it is hard to see how any of us will enter heaven without being reconciled to all our brothers and sisters: 'If you come to offer your gift on the altar and there find that your brother or sister has something against you, go first and be reconciled with them and then come and offer your gift' (Mt 5).

Does this mean that we can leave reconciliation to the next life? No. The longer we leave reconciliation the more harm we do to ourselves and others, and the more hurt we cause to God. Secondly, it is clear from the scriptures that we are called to make a basic response to God in this life. However, where this response has not led to complete reconciliation we can still hope that the desperation of the Mother will find some way to draw us out of isolation, while still respecting our freedom.

It is obvious that complete reconciliation is not actually achieved in this life. Many of us do not use the talents God gave us to the full. All of us, in some sense, are part of unjust structures. Given this, what does God do? Does she wave a magic wand over us and cure our brokenness? Is this not the temptation that Jesus faced constantly during his life, the temptation not to take our freedom fully seriously? Our task in the next life remains the same although the context will be very different: to enter freely into a relationship, mirroring that of the three Persons with each other, with every person and community in the world.

What follows from this is that our journey towards growth in community does not stop when we leave this world. The tares remain to be separated from the wheat. Certainly it will be very different from this world. Yet the task to be done, and our capacity to resist it, will surely remain similar. In this context the Catholic notion of purgatory, which is very difficult for many Protestants, is of central importance. It is the process through which, by grace, we may face our reality in a new way and grow towards both forgiveness and reconciliation.

There are probably not too many people in Northern Ireland who believe in the possibility of universal salvation. Many of those who believe in being 'born again' will have problems with it. The idea that all might be saved is at variance with a society which places great stress on exclusivism. Its challenge is that if we are going to have to live together as a condition of being part of God's community in the next life, then we had better learn how to do so in this. We may choose to kill each other but the bodies of our victims will rise up to confront us at the gates of heaven. We shall not enter those gates without being reconciled. And there are more ways of killing people than through violence.

If we want to follow Christ then a response to the emphasis on universalism in the gospels is needed at both a personal and a communal level. If people do not want to follow Christ then they are better off saying that. The people that Our Lord had the greatest difficulty with were those who claimed to love God, but who did not do so in practice.

Conclusion
In this and the past three chapters I have outlined what I see as some of the central statements that we can make about the Christian God. If these statements were taken seriously what kind of challenges would they raise for us? The remainder of this book is an attempt to answer this question, but before moving on it may be worthwhile to outline in a table the sort of demands that may arise.

Theological Statement	Type of response needed
1. God is a God of community	No individualism; respect for diversity; search for the mystery of God in other communities; building community becomes the task of Christians .
2. God liberates	God is to be found in the human struggle for liberation, especially with economically deprived people.
3. God is inclusive	God's community is about building respect and communication among diverse and often opposed groups. It can be measured by the extent of power and respect given to the poor, women, foreigners and people that society regards as outcasts. It asks us what we mean by the phrase 'one of ours'.
4. God reconciles	In God's community the task of seeking and offering forgiveness is of crucial importance to members, both as individuals and as groups.
5. God is involved in conflict	God's community will not avoid conflict if it is necessary for the sake of justice; but Christians will very rarely be open to being violent; they will avoid self-righteousness.
6. God suffers and fails	Failure, rejection and suffering will often be experienced by God's community. Christians are called to stand alongside sinners and to do so while being aware of their own sinfulness. Jesus was a victim but he remained free and therefore powerful.
7. God triumphs	Christians will have a deep hope that God's community is being established and that it will be fully revealed in time. But in this hope they will not pretend that present day suffering and injustice are unimportant. Nor will they be fatalistic about them. They will hope for universal salvation and treat others as people with whom they are called to share eternal life.

SECTION III
A task for the Catholic Church

CHAPTER 7

Worship and sacraments

The picture we have found in the scriptures is of a God centred on community. It was to bring about a community that would reflect the life of the three Persons that the Son became one of us. It is the task of the Christian community to live as witnesses to this community, thereby encouraging others to do the same, and hastening the day when the world will be fully reconciled to God.

There are two general ways in which Catholics can become part of God's community – or fail to do so. One is in the way we live as church. The second is as members of society. These two ways are closely linked.

Firstly, they are linked because of the need for credibility. If the church wants to see reconciliation and justice in society at large then it needs to show that these exist within its own boundaries. Otherwise people will simply not take it seriously.

Secondly, they are linked because our relationships within the church have an effect on the attitudes, values and energy that we bring to society. So, if reconciliation and justice are priorities for us because of our understanding of God's community, and if we live out of these values within the church, then this inevitably will influence the way we practise politics. But if we act unjustly towards one another within the church then this will lessen the creative energy we bring to society and also block us from seeing what is wrong with society.

Thirdly, interchurch relations influence the potential of all churches to help the growth of reconciliation and justice in society as a whole. In the context of Northern Ireland, divisions among the churches reinforce the political and secular divisions that exist. We have inherited a tragic history in which our ancestors were divided across a range of issues, including religion. But because we have inherited these divisions we are faced with the task of responding to them. Our response can, either by accident or design, continue and reinforce these divisions and thereby pass on even deeper problems to those who follow us. Or we can tackle the divisions and pass on interchurch relations radically different from those we have received.

In this context we need to look at what might be termed 'ordinary church work', that is celebrating the sacraments, and building community through church-linked bodies. In other parts of the world where there is political consensus, such work often helps people to develop a positive religious identity. This in turn enables them to make a contribution to the wider society. But in Northern Ireland people are divided in their housing, jobs, schools, interpretation of history, attitude to the state, and political loyalties. This produces a separateness that is lethal. In these circumstances, churches need to be very careful about what they mean when they say they are building 'community'. Is it a separate church community which adds to the divisions that already exist in society? Or is it a church community whose aim and practice is to reduce such divisions? In the Northern Ireland context it is not over-dramatic to say that this is a matter of life and death.

In this situation, therefore, an important principle should be applied: when there is tension over important religious values then churches should opt for the interpretation which will enhance relationships in the interests of peace and reconciliation, and ultimately of life itself.[1]

What this principle suggests is that there are many areas of thinking within the church where one can lean towards one or other interpretation. Either may be possible. What are the factors that influence us in choosing one or other? In the context of Northern Ireland part of that answer should be the overwhelming need for reconciliation and justice, so that we may be part of God's community, and not isolated from it.

The degree to which the church responds to its calling to be a sign of God's community in the world is the degree to which it will be in touch with God. It needs to make the building of community an absolute priority. It cannot be an image of God unless in some way it reflects the community of three Persons that God is. This involves being a community centred on the tasks of liberation, of being inclusive, seeking forgiveness and reconciliation with our enemies, being willing to face up to conflict when necessary, being open to taking on the suffering that preaching the word involves, and being infused with a deep hope based on the joy of the risen Lord.

In the particular context of Northern Ireland the church needs to apply these ideals constructively and creatively to a situation in which there are two minorities, two groups of people suffering, each depending in some way on outside powers, who themselves have an ambiguous relationship with each other and with the groups within Northern Ireland.

Clearly no Christian community lives up to this ideal. Further, ideals can be disempowering if they are too far beyond us, or if they are simply impossible given our actual practical situation. However, we can sometimes respond to this by toning down the ideal and by adjusting it to fit into our present, visible situation. That is the tyranny of the present. It is making God fit into our own categories, trimming him down to our size. It is a sin of which we are all too often guilty in Northern Ireland.

Instead of doing this we need to challenge constantly our own ideas of who God is, because God is always a mystery, deeper than any of our thoughts.

In this chapter I want to take each of the theological themes that I have outlined and raise a series of questions about our response.

1. GOD IS A GOD OF COMMUNITY
Eucharist
The eucharist is a central issue because it is so important in Catholic life, both at the level of theology, and at a more popular level. One is a good Catholic, so many will say, if one goes to Mass on a Sunday, and not otherwise. This is an impoverished notion of what it is to be a Catholic, but it means that the eucharist could act as a trigger issue: changing the way we understand and practise it could lead to changes in other areas of the church. In fact opening people up to what the eucharist is really about would transform the Catholic community of Ireland. It would turn our focus away from a privatised and other-worldly religion into a lively faith that was centred on building God's community here and now, especially with those who are our enemies. There is in practice no more urgent task facing the Irish church than to transform the popular understanding of what it means to take part in the eucharist and the consequences of this for our lives.

a) The eucharist and the formation of the Christian community
At the eucharist we remember what Our Lord did at the Last Supper. But the English term 'remember' does not convey what Our Lord would have meant by that term. For the Jewish people it meant much more than it does to us today.

The context in which the Last Supper took place was that of a Passover Meal. This was the annual celebration in which the Jews remembered the event that made them into a people: the Exodus experience in which God liberated them from slavery in Egypt. But they did not remember this event simply as something in the past. Rather, by participating in the sacred meal they were caught up in what God had done to their ancestors. More than this: they believed that whatever God did to their ancestors he did to themselves. The reason for this was that they had a very strong notion of being one people. This was so strong that they identified themselves with Moses and the Prophets. So when they came to remember the exodus experience at the Passover meal they entered once again into the same relationship that their ancestors had with God: people who were freed from slavery.

The way that they remembered their past was what formed the Jews into a community. Through their memory of this past they became present to both their ancestors and their God. They experienced themselves as a people given to God.

All this is the background to Jesus's injunction to us at the Last Supper: 'Do this in memory of me'. What it means is that the Lord is telling us to celebrate a special supper and through that to be caught up and made present to what he himself did at the Last Supper when he gave himself to his Father on our behalf. That offering was lived out on the cross the day after the Last Supper. The eucharist, then, is the sacramental event that moulds us into God's people.

b) The eucharist as the Body of Christ

The Eucharist is about the Body of Christ. That has two, closely related, meanings. One is that it is a central means by which we are brought into contact with Christ, who is the historical Jesus. The second is that we are brought into contact with Christ, who, in a certain sense, *is* his community. Christ makes the identity between himself and his community so close that he can say, 'As often as you do this to one of the least of my brethren you do it me' (Mt 25). When we partake in the eucharist, then, we receive the body, the person, of the historical Christ. We are made part of his offering to his Father. But we also receive his community. We are made part of it. Our union with his community is deepened.

Who belongs to Christ's community? For some the answer is those who are present in the church taking part in the eucharist. But Jesus Christ did not live and die only for Catholics, especially since we know that he lived and died as a Jew. He did not simply live and die for those who were later to become his followers. He lived and died for everyone born into the world. Unless our eucharist reflects that reality in some tangible way it is not likely to bring alive its connection with the Last Supper.

Secondly, if we take part in the eucharist we commit ourselves to building relationships with others and especially with our enemies. That is one consequence of being given to God as one people by Christ. To take part in the eucharist and at the same time to have no serious intention to do work at our relationships, both as individuals and as a community, is to commit blasphemy. It is to misuse a gift of God. It is to be engaged in a pretence. It is on the one hand to say at Mass: we give ourselves to God with Christ and with everyone else in the world, because Christ died that all might be saved; and on the other hand to say that we will continue to harbour enmity, and that we will make no effort to build just relationships. If such is our attitude we may well be physically present at Mass, we may even physically receive the sacred host, but we are not in touch with our God, because we have separated ourselves from his community; as individuals, and perhaps as a community, we fail to reflect God's community.

2. GOD LIBERATES

Economically deprived people

The eucharist is a means by which we can be drawn into God's liberating and reconciling activity. It is difficult to see how people can read the gospels without being struck by Christ's concern for and involvement with those who were economically deprived. Yet in practice some people seem to be able to go to Mass regularly and at the same time to feel no great anger at economic divisions in society. John O'Brien puts this well: '... how is it that people who support consumerism, individualism, class distinction and are not significantly moved by the issues of unemployment, patriarchy, injustice and the Third World seem to experience little difficulty in being regular Mass attenders?'[2] Many people seem happy enough to believe that they are part of God's community because they commit no great sins. Yet they forget the central role that Jesus gave to those who were deprived. These people are right that God will always love them. The covenant means in part that from God's side her attitude to us will always be one of deepening love. What many forget is that if deprived people are unable to recognise them on the last day, they in turn will not be able to recognise God, because the Christian God is a God of the deprived.

They also forget that being silent involves taking a stance. Our greatest sins are probably those of omission. It is our silence that allows the status quo, in which the deprived are boxed into an unjust situation, to continue.

The priest, in the story of the Good Samaritan, did no harm to the man who was robbed. He simply walked by on the far side. Similarly the rich man did no harm to Lazarus. He simply ignored him. By failing to act as neighbours to those whom they met both the priest and the rich man put themselves outside God's community.

It is this insight that lies behind the idea that the church must make an option for the poor. If we do not work for reconciliation between rich and poor, how can we be credible in working for it between Catholic and Protestant? If our notion of God's community extends to Protestants, but not to the economically deprived in both the Catholic and Protestant community, how can we be confident that we are in touch with God?

Working with economically deprived people to bring about a more equal distribution of wealth inevitably involves conflict. One source of this is the resistance of better-off people because of their own vested interests. A second comes from groups who are themselves deprived. Their resistance is an example of the horizontal oppression to which Paolo Freire refers. It comes partly from the insecurity engendered by some people in the community making economic progress, and partly because they have internalised many of the attitudes of the dominant economic group.

An example of conflict was the disagreements during the IRA campaign between some lay groups and Catholic priests over control of British Government funding for unemployment schemes. The British Government sometimes used the Catholic clergy as a channel for funding such projects because they believed this would ensure that funds would not be misappropriated by paramilitaries. But it also meant that clergy were being given – and were taking on – power over such schemes. There was a dilemma here for clergy because they also wanted to ensure that money was not misappropriated, but it was a major drawback that through these schemes clergy took on power, as distinct from influence. It is almost always preferable that lay people, and especially those who are more economically deprived, run projects like these.

Catholic clergy for the most part come from a middle class background. The number of working class people that we have persuaded to join us is extremely low. In these circumstances it is all the more important for us to make serious efforts to understand the life experience of people who are deprived.

We need solid and respectful links with people who live in deprived areas. While it is impossible for those of us who have never been unemployed to understand fully the feelings of those who are, nonetheless some insight can be gained both from listening to people and from going on short experiences that involve deprivation. This need for understanding works both ways. Those who have never had steady work, and whose income has therefore always been low, will need to work hard to understand the experiences, for example, of business people who face cash flow problems and whose house mortgages are thereby threatened.

If people living in deprived areas look at parish groups and find them dominated only by middle-class people, if they also know the petty superiority with which some middle-class people look down on those more deprived (often a pathetic case of the pot calling the kettle black), why should they get involved in such groups? Even if they do, will these groups be dominated by a middle-class or working-class culture? (An easy way to answer this to ask how shocked the group will be by so-called bad language).

One way to check where we stand in relation to justice for economically deprived people is to ask: are all our friends middle-class? If they are, then we need to develop deeper friendships with working-class people.

Non-violence

All over the world the Irish have a reputation for violence. Most of this, in the past twenty-five years, comes from the conflict in the north. It is a major block to opening up non-Christian areas of the world to the riches of Christianity, because their image of Ireland is one of violence. Irish churches have a mammoth task to change this image.

What is needed is not speeches and sermons, but serious discussions about our anger, our political objectives, our frustrations, the behaviour of the security forces, and how we can act non-violently. Christians in Ireland need to be convinced both of the gospel value and the practicality of non-violence. In saying this I am not thinking only of paramilitaries, but of many staunch members of churches in Northern Ireland who can see no other response to violence than counter-violence.

It is extraordinary that in a situation of such prolonged conflict Irish Christians have not developed a spirituality as rich as that of Gandhi or of Martin Luther King, arising out of our own context. The reason we have not done so is simple: we have so often decided not to pay the price of costly reconciliation.

3. GOD IS INCLUSIVE

Intercommunion

I have already touched on the issue of inclusiveness when I discussed the issue of the community that we have in mind when we celebrate the eucharist. Related to this is the question of whom we admit to the eucharist and whom we exclude. Vatican II, in its *Decree on Ecumenism* (par 8), says that since the eucharist is a sign of unity, intercommunion (*communicatio in sacris* refers to this among other things) is therefore normally not allowed where such unity does not already exist. However, it goes on in the very next sentence to say that the eucharist is also a means of grace, and, as such, intercommunion is sometimes to be commended. Later legislation in the church has specified the occasions on which such eucharistic sharing is to be allowed. I remarked once that they amount to 'chance encounters in the Sahara desert with wandering Presbyterians who happen to believe in reservation of the eucharist' – in other words, practically never.[3]

However, our theology, and therefore our legislation, is constantly changing and this has affected the issue of intercommunion. The 1993 *Directory on Ecumenism* confirms that the local bishop, in consultation with the episcopal conference, can establish general norms for judging 'situations of grave and pressing need' (par 130). Is not the situation in Northern Ireland a context of 'grave and pressing need'? We shall see in a moment that the Directory is deliberately vague on the issue of intercommunion in mixed marriages, apparently in order to be less restrictive. It is surely incumbent on us in our Irish context to use whatever flexibility the law gives us in order to advance the cause of reconciliation and of justice.

The issue of intercommunion is, however, a highly emotive one. This is not surprising. The eucharist is at the centre of our church's life and practice. It is natural therefore that many will react with deep emotion to any suggested change, whether or not they support a restrictive view of intercommunion. Further, such feelings about the importance of the eucharist are compounded by our reactions as members of a community that has been hurt. Because of this hurt we often feel resentment towards people in other churches. Reconciliation work is not about trying to avoid such feelings, or pretending that they do not exist.

Given the depth of feelings that we can have, we may well need a fair bit of prayer to allow us to be open to the arguments for and against intercommunion. Otherwise we may end up with either too restrictive a practice, or else a false liberalism that suggests it is an

unimportant question. Either response would not be a help to reconciliation and justice.

Having said that, we need to look at inconsistencies in our practice on intercommunion. At the moment divorced Catholics who
are living in a second relationship without their first marriage having been annulled are officially excluded from the eucharist. So are
non-members of the Roman Catholic Church, except members of
Orthodox churches. Why exclude these and not others, for example, paramilitaries? It might be argued that the church has been
vehement and consistent in condemning the use of paramilitary
violence, and that anyone involved in such activity should therefore exclude themselves from the eucharist. This is correct, but
there is still a difference between this case and the other examples
where the church, by its rules, bars people from participation.

The importance of this issue is that it lies within our power as
Catholics to do something about it. The Catholic Church in Ireland
has particular reasons for questioning this legislation. If the eucharist
is a means of grace – and it surely is – then we, of all people in the
world, need to have this recognised. In a situation where many
Protestants are understandably hurt at the refusal of the Catholic
Church to recognise the validity of their ministry, offering eucharistic hospitality would be a healing gesture. Why then do we not
allow intercommunion in certain circumstances in order to help
reconciliation?

Making ecumenism more central to the life of the church
There is a wider issue that affects ecumenism as a whole. That is the
question of how we move it from a situation where it is peripheral
to the life of both communities, to a point where it could make an
impact on the ordinary worship of the community. If building community is the central task of the Christian, then making ecumenism
central to the life of the church is also vital. This cannot happen as
long as we confine it to events like Church Unity Octave, which are
always seen as optional extras, or, even worse, as the dues that we
owe to the ecumenical movement: having paid our dues we can
then ignore reconciliation for the rest of the year and get on with the
real life of the church – which is always seen as being concerned
only with its own members.

Until our focus moves from our own broken and limited section
of God's community to God's community as a whole, we will never
do much to reflect the community that the three Persons share with
each other.

One small way of helping to make reconciliation more central in the ordinary life of the church would be to invite Protestant clergy to give witness during Mass. Of course there are difficulties with this suggestion. Many Protestant clergy would resist such a prospect because their congregations would prevent them, or because they still think that the Catholic Church believes it repeats the sacrifice of Calvary, or, in some cases, because they think the church is the anti-Christ referred to in the Book of Revelation. But there are clergy who would be open to such a suggestion.

If sharing pulpits is considered too difficult, why not share readers? This is allowed by the 1993 Directory 'in exceptional cases or for a just cause' (par 133). Ecumenical work in Northern Ireland, as elsewhere, is about the art of the possible. But if it is not possible to share even readers one has to ask why? What does this say about the Christian – and therefore ecumenical – commitment of one or of both the communities involved?

4. GOD RECONCILES

Interchurch marriages

Conflict between churches over interchurch marriages is less than it used to be. Two changes in the Catholic Church have helped. One is that all Catholics, whether they are getting married to a non-Roman Catholic or not, are asked to promise to do all in their power to bring the children up as Catholics. This means that those entering mixed marriages are treated no differently from other Catholics. However, at least as important is the change in the understanding of what the promise means. In 1977 the Bishops of England and Wales in their new *Directory on Mixed Marriages* made it clear that Catholics in mixed marriages had to follow a certain priority in their obligations. First, they had to respect the unity of the marriage; second, they had to respect the religious views and rights of their partner; third, within that context, they had to do all they could to bring the children up as Catholics. That same priority has now been adopted by the Irish Bishops, and the promise that all Catholics are asked to take is worded to that effect. The 1993 Directory also makes clear that the primary concern of the church, in all marriages, is to uphold the union of the couple (par 144).

A further change is that it is now easier for a Catholic to get permission to be married in a Protestant church, with the minister acting as official witness instead of a priest. From an ecumenical point of view, it is often easier if the wedding takes place in a Protestant church. This is because of the difficulties many Protestants have, for doctrinal or political reasons, in attending Catholic churches.

Generally, also, a Protestant wedding will not have a eucharist, which means that, in the context of current Roman Catholic legislation, the problem of intercommunion will not arise. But it should be noted that the 1993 Directory is deliberately vague about the issue of intercommunion for interchurch couples (cf par 159). It is reasonable to conclude that the purpose of this vagueness is so that practice will not be over-restrictive. Again, one hopes that the Irish bishops will be generous in allowing intercommunion for these couples.

Both as part of the mixed marriage issue, and for its own sake, there could easily be greater ecumenical co-operation in baptism. All the mainline Christian churches recognise each other's baptism. Thus a person who, for example, is baptised in the Church of Ireland, cannot be re-baptised if he or she were to join the Roman Catholic Church. The fact that some churches may disagree about the appropriateness of infant baptism does not change this. Yet, despite this, baptism can be a source of division between the churches. The reason for this is that one is not only baptised into the universal church of Christ, but also into a particular denomination. Thus baptism is one of the stumbling blocks interchurch couples face in their obstacle-course relationship with the churches.

Ideally, clergy from both churches should be present at baptisms of children of mixed marriages, whether these are held in the Catholic Church or in other churches. Obviously the Catholic Church would prefer if the child were baptised as a Catholic, but the same is true in reverse for other churches. If reconciliation is a priority, we should rejoice that the child is becoming a member of the full Christian community and respect the decision of the parents who have to make the best choice they can. It is not the fault of the parents that the churches are divided.

The sacrament of reconciliation

Of all the sacraments, reconciliation cries out for an emphasis to be placed on political and social reconciliation. There have been important changes in the sacrament in the Catholic Church in recent years. One of the most significant is that the number of people availing of it has declined. That is a pity. The sacrament is a particular way in which individuals and communities can experience the forgiveness of the Lord in a tangible way, express their sorrow for sin, and commit themselves once again to new life. Undoubtedly, one of the blocks for many people is the individualistic type of spirituality which has become popular with many. For these people the idea of expressing repentance for one's sins to the community, or of the community seeking forgiveness, makes little sense, because they can only think of their relationship with God in individualistic terms.

A second block is a false liberalism which emphasises the forgiveness that God in Christ offers us, but overlooks or neglects the anger that God experiences at our sins, because they do wrong to the sisters and brothers of Christ.

One of the good liturgical changes that has taken place is new ways of celebrating the sacrament, ways that emphasise its communal aspects. Such celebrations are particularly important at times like Christmas, and especially Easter. But here, as with other events in the life of the church, one has to ask why is the sacrament not celebrated ecumenically? Many Protestants, of course, will have doctrinal difficulties with the sacrament. But that is not the point. Why do Catholics not seek out those Protestant clergy who are open to the sacrament, in order that a fuller expression of the church of Christ may be present when we come to celebrate it? It would be entirely appropriate in any ecumenical programme between churches if its high points were at the great celebrations of the churches' liturgical year: the incarnation at Christmas and the paschal feast at Easter. It would be fitting if, as part of those celebrations, Protestant ministers were present during the large communal acts of repentance by the Catholic community. Such ministers, from a different tradition of the church of Christ, could contribute to communal efforts to examine our conscience and in particular point to sins of omission which we often commit because of a lack of awareness of the suffering we cause, or of the opportunities for reconciliation that we ignore. They could lead the community in prayers to seek forgiveness, and they could encourage us by their own personal and communal experience of that forgiveness. One would hope that the same thing could happen in some Protestant churches, but, even without this, Catholic clergy should take the lead, because reconciliation has to be our priority.

The sacrament of reconciliation could also quite naturally lead to communal acts of repentance. These could play an important role in the process of healing. But there are no easy answers as to when or how repentance should be expressed. It needs to be done at the right time, in the right way, by the right people. It is impossible to know in advance when a gesture meets these criteria. This is true of all symbolic actions. Gandhi's salt march did not seem particularly important at first. It was only as people began to interpret it that it took on greater significance.

The church can help people to look at the issue of communal

repentance. What should the Catholic community, north and south, repent for? How should it do it? When? Most of the answers we come up with will inevitably have to be discarded for one reason or another. But we may in time choose useful gestures, if we are committed enough to stay at prayer and discernment long enough to find them.

Other sacraments

Other sacraments, such as confirmation and ordination, could also be part of an ecumenical programme between churches. A very simple idea is to invite Protestant clergy to attend post-confirmation dinners, a custom already being practised in some parishes. Quite frequently clergy from different churches are invited to attend each other's ceremonies of induction into new parishes or congregations. It is important on these occasions to help strangers to feel at home.

There is a need for all mainline churches to be represented officially at each other's ceremonies, because we are brothers and sisters in the Lord. This may not be possible on a frequent basis because of time constraints but it should take place at least on major feasts during the year. If no effort is made to achieve this then one has to ask what is the church's priority: to build separate communities, or to build an open, reconciled community? The question here is not necessarily how successful our efforts are to make our celebrations ecumenical (often Protestant opposition is strong enough to defeat such efforts) but rather how much effort we give to this task.

The role of clergy

A major task for clergy in Northern Ireland is to be leaders in the struggle for reconciliation, and its co-relative, justice. It is vital that we begin to see this work of peace-making as the most important part of our calling. We are only a section of the church, but if we became convinced about the importance of peace-making we could have an extraordinarily positive impact on the wider community.

Clergy can play a particularly important role in communicating the fears of our own community to other churches. We can do this not only through clergy fraternals, but also by setting up inter-church groups. We need to trust people a lot before we will tell them our fears. Building up this trust is one of the most important tasks of reconciliation because there is so much fear in Northern Ireland.

If clergy are to work effectively at reconciliation and justice we need to be trained for it. There is an assumption that because we study philosophy and theology, and possibly also a secular discipline, we can therefore take on all the tasks involved in parish or priestly work. But reconciliation work with groups that we may resent, or even not feel confident with, is not easy. Clergy are not statues. We are human beings with our own inadequacies, failures and fears. Reconciliation and justice work in Northern Ireland is particularly difficult. There are a myriad of pressures against it: the feelings of the community to which we belong, as well as our own feelings, the blocks in the Protestant community, the demands of political justice, the possibility that even if we analyse a problem correctly we may respond in the wrong way or at the wrong time. Because of this, on-going training is important. Taking courses at the Irish School of Ecumenics would be helpful. So would spending some time abroad, because often it is only by standing back from our situation and comparing it with that in other countries that we can see it in a new light.

It is easy to think of Catholic priests who have made a serious contribution to justice. One thinks of the work of John Murphy, chaplain in Long Kesh throughout the 1981 hunger strikes and still chaplain thirteen years later (his ministry is often appreciated as much by Protestant as by Catholic prisoners); of Denis Faul, who has campaigned with extraordinary energy on behalf of people who have been wrongly convicted and also against abuses by the security forces; of Ray Murray who challenged so many of the killings carried out by the SAS.

It may be invidious to mention particular individuals because there are many others involved in similar work who are less well known. But there are not enough priests involved in this type of work and the example of some should spur others on.

We also need to ask to what extent our work for justice is only for members of the Catholic community or to what extent it is denominationally blind. Reconciliation and justice have to go together. One criterion by which to test whether our justice is reconciling or not is to ask how much the concerns of the Protestant as well as the Catholic community figure in our agenda.

The role of religious congregations
Religious orders have also been involved in the work of reconciliation and justice. The Redemptorists in Clonard monastery have carried on a ministry in the centre of West Belfast since they moved to

the north in 1896. They have been closely involved in the concerns of local people. Their annual novena of prayer has a very strong ecumenical thrust, with both Protestant preachers included and many Protestants attending. Alex Reid played a crucial role in helping to bring about the IRA ceasefire in 1994. Other Redemptorists have been involved in the reconciliation work of Corrymeela and of the Cornerstone community. Many of these initiatives took place in times of very high tension following killings, and priests from religious orders were often involved in negotiations between extremely angry mourners and the RUC at the funerals of paramilitaries.

Other religious have spent many years living and actively involved in very deprived areas, especially in Belfast. Many of these religious are women. Much of their work has been on community development issues, especially in trying to build confidence among local women. They have also either been open to, or committed to, building ecumenical contacts from within their local communities. Their work is based on a vision of God's community, similar to what lies behind this book.

This work of justice and reconciliation has not been confined to people living in more deprived areas, but has also been carried on by other religious working in more traditional ministries, such as education and hospitals.

Finally, it is worth mentioning one task that is needed in Northern Ireland and with which clergy in all churches might be able to help: desegregating housing. At the end of 1994, over 50% of the people of Northern Ireland lived in areas with less than a 10% presence of the other tradition. This segregation has come about as a response to paramilitary attacks. It increases the ignorance that each group has of the other. Desegregating housing is far more important and basic than integrating education, because cross-community educational contact is more difficult in the context of segregated housing. Churches could do a lot to ensure that people from other religions are made welcome in an area and to ensure that they are protected from attacks and vandalism. They could also play a part in developing housing policies to encourage desegregation.

5. GOD IS INVOLVED IN CONFLICT

I have argued that two of the reasons why the church needs to look at its own record in regard to reconciliation and justice are because of the need for credibility and because of the new energy we can experience by being a reconciled community. This is particularly true in regard to two issues: the marginalisation of women, and disputes over the way authority is exercised.

The marginalisation of women in the church

Good feminism is a critique of discrimination with all its attendant abuse of power and relationships. This critique is not about replacing men with women in the present structures within the church. It is about changing the way men and women relate to each other and the way that power and authority are exercised. Feminism very often bridges social and cultural gaps in a way that few other issues can. Women who have utterly different interests can find an instinctive bond with each other because they recognise each other's experience of oppression in a way that is difficult for many men to do.

What is perhaps surprising about this issue is that many northern Catholics can instinctively and quite properly respond with anger to examples of discrimination against themselves, but at the same time often be blind to discrimination against women within the church. This in part is because so much energy is drained by the nationalist-unionist conflict. Catholic women in the north do not seem to be particularly sensitive to feminist issues, especially in the church. When they criticise the church it is often for political, rather than feminist, reasons. Men are often slow to understand the pain of women. Reflecting on this reality might help northern Irish Catholic men to understand why, in a different form of discrimination, unionists have often been so slow to believe that Catholics were being oppressed. The dynamics of discrimination, and the responses to it, tend to be similar for all groups.

A simple example is that of sexist language. Some women find this offensive. They do not think, for example, that the words 'mankind' and 'men' should be used to refer to both men and women. To use a phrase such as 'men and women' does not alter the meaning of prayers. So why do people resist a change towards more inclusive language?

An analogy might be the use of the term 'British' to refer to all the people of Northern Ireland. Catholics would rightly object to such a practice because they are not British. On the same basis, it seems reasonable to make our language, especially in our liturgy, more inclusive. It is interesting to note the way some people respond to this by using the argument of tradition: we have always used 'mankind', so we should continue to do so. But the same people would immediately reject an argument based on tradition in other situations, for example, to justify Orange marches going through nationalist areas!

Other issues raised by many Catholic women are: the way the

tradition presents women, especially the Mother of God, as obedient and self-sacrificing; the emphasis on family life by the church which sometimes means that the role of single women is often overlooked; the teaching of *Humanae Vitae* on artificial contraception, which is rejected by many; the degree of effort that is put into opposing abortion compared with the comparative silence about violence against women.

The church needs to listen much more carefully to women who believe that they are marginalised by it. Such listening is not easy when there is so much pain. Clergy need to avoid any hint of arrogance or paternalism in sermons or in church statements. We need to look at the psychological reasons behind some of the opposition to the ordination of women. We need to challenge men to take proper responsibility for their role in fathering children. We need to stress the equal responsibility that men have for the rearing and nurturing of children. We need to challenge insecure male stereotypes. We need to place as much emphasis on rape and other forms of violence against women as we do on abortion and contraception. We also need to give much greater space to the role that experience and emotions necessarily play in the moral positions that the church adopts.

This last sentence is in itself revealing. Who are the 'we' who are to look at the concerns of women? Men! Or so it seems, because it is men and men only who exercise authority within the church. That is because women are barred from ordination, and authority within the church is currently exercised exclusively by those who are ordained. It is not easy to see how women can be allowed to exercise a charism of authority in the church as long as they are not ordained. Whether we like it or not, then, the reasons why women are excluded from ordination will continue to be debated by loyal Catholics, and some of these will continue to find the arguments unconvincing.

But quite apart from the issue of ordination, there are other ways in which women could be more involved in the life of the church. Examples are: giving witness at Mass, and putting their concerns as women, young and old, married, single, or separated, before a congregation; giving greater scope to the many trained women theologians in Ireland whose skills could be used by any diocese in the education of both laity and clergy. This has already happened to a degree, but much more could be done. This can only happen if parishes and dioceses are prepared to make it a priority, which means paying people for their services, especially as some lay theologians have no other source of income. We could also look at new ways of involving non-ordained people, especially women, in decision-making in the church. For example, African Bishop Ernest Kembo at the 1994 Synod of Bishops called for women to be made 'lay cardinals'.

Is there a connection between the role of women in the church and our central question of how Catholics can contribute to reconciliation and justice in Northern Ireland? I believe the two are intimately connected. What has come to me in the course of writing this book is the extent to which we need to change our relationships within the church, firstly in order to come closer to the model of relationships that exist within the Trinity, and, secondly, if we are to make a constructive impact on the world in which we live and to which we are called to bear witness. If the dominant theme of the Catholic Church, as well as of the other churches, was on the central importance of reconciliation and justice, as two elements of the one reality, then church members would change and thereby change the way that we think and act politically.

Those who have been conscientised by feminism are aware of the way women have been and continue to be oppressed by men and of the crucial need for a more inclusive church. This, in turn, naturally raises issues of justice, forgiveness and reconciliation. Without a new relationship between men and women within the church, it is unlikely that the church in Northern Ireland will be able to face the demands of the gospels in a divided society.

The exercise of authority
Throughout history the way that authority has been exercised in the church has often been a source of conflict. This is still the case today. The issue is important to any discussion of reconciliation because the way that we exercise authority can be a sign of the degree to which we live in a reconciled and just manner.

There are deep disagreements within the Catholic Church on many issues: the ordination of women, the use of artificial contraception, infallibility, the status of non-Roman Catholic ministry, and intercommunion, to name but a few. What matters in these is: what is the truth? The answer to any such question is unlikely to be final. Truth is something that emerges continuously, slowly and painfully. It needs dialogue. It is vital within the church that we develop means to encourage such dialogue. It would greatly help if there was less censorship and a greater appreciation of the role to be played by 'loyal dissent'.

A second reason why such discussion is important is that Protestants would understand more easily some of the differences that we Catholics have. One of the continuing ecumenical problems is that so many Protestants know nothing of our disagreements. They therefore think of Catholics as a strong, monolithic group. Since many see us also as being opposed to Protestantism, they fear us greatly. It would ease their fears if we let them know more of our truth, by being more open about our disagreements.

6. GOD SUFFERS AND FAILS

Spirituality

Spirituality is at the heart of the life of any church. It is the point where theology, prayer, worship and life experience all interact. It is also the deepest layer in the community so that it is hard to tease out the true pattern of spirituality that influences a community, as distinct from what people think are the dominant themes.

One element of spirituality about which we need to be careful within the Catholic Church is that of the victim. Christ was a victim. So are many Catholic/nationalists within Northern Ireland. But Christ's response to suffering was one of passionate understanding of, and forgiveness for, his oppressors. He also relativised all political solutions to oppression. Further, Catholics are not the only victims in Northern Ireland. They, like Protestants, are victims because of the flawed relationship that exists between them. Christ's response as a victim was not simply to state how he was being oppressed, but to confront his oppressors, to offer them forgiveness and to seek a new relationship with them. His failure to achieve this caused him to weep over Jerusalem, but it did not stop him from pleading on their behalf on the cross.

There is still a strong element of spirituality among northern nationalists that echoes the experience of the penal laws and of the famine. This is because nationalists continue to experience oppression today. But there is a need to balance this sense of being a victim with one of responsibility for the future. The people of the exodus gained their freedom because they responded to God's offer to leave their slavery. Jesus suffered failure in his own life, yet his mission was a success because at the centre of his being he remained free. As Catholics we cannot force Protestants or the British state to enter into a new relationship with us. But we can open ourselves to a new relationship even if others do not respond. In practice this tends to draw others into relationship. It is only by offering and seeking a new relationship with the Protestant/British community that our oppression – and theirs – will end. This process is somewhat parallel to what happens when we respond to God's grace, which is always given prior to any response on our part.

Our prayers for freedom and a new relationship should not be passive. Rather, we should pray like the slave who asked for his freedom year after year. There was no response to his prayer from God, until one day the prayer ran down into his legs and he ran away.[4] Prayer should free us to act.

We need to ask what kind of spirituality we are trying to develop. Does it encourage people to move from self-pity to working to develop new relationships? Is it escapist or incarnational? Is it one that is centred on this life, where Christ is to be found, or on the next life where he is to be found only by those who have gone there? Is it one that leads to action? Does it encourage self-righteousness and the scapegoating of others? Does it relate to the real needs of people? Does it challenge as well as comfort people? Does it face people with the need to build just relationships with those who were deprived? Does it help people to move on the long road of seeking and offering forgiveness for hurts given and received?

There is every reason why spirituality must be ecumenical. Catholics have no exclusive hold on prayer. Particularly at times of retreats or missions in parishes, asking for the help of Christians in other denominations can be a powerful witness to the unity that we already share, as well as a means of making use of the experience and insights of others. Clergy could give the lead in this by asking for Protestant ministers – both male and female – to help out at our own annual retreats.

A prayer experience that we found useful in Portadown was a week of prayer adapted from the Spiritual Exercises of St Ignatius. Lay people found it particularly helpful. Those invited to take part were often not enthusiastic church attenders. This meant that these weeks of prayer did not get the reputation of being only for the pious. Secondly, there was a natural and appropriate involvement of non-Roman Catholics both in leading and in taking part in these weeks.

7. GOD TRIUMPHS

God triumphs when Christ's community of respect, reconciliation and justice is being established. None of us can be sure that the way we live and work is in accordance with this ideal. In fact we can presumably be sure of the opposite: that our prejudices, fears and failures are a constant block to it. But God is not limited by our destructiveness. We should therefore look for ways in which God is at work drawing us into just relationships with each other. If our priority is reconciliation and justice then we will look for these in changes in our liturgies, in our interchurch relations, in the place given to deprived people in our own community, and in a growing sensitivity and response to the sense of exclusion experienced by many women. The triumph of the church will be shown in deeper and more respectful relationships both within the church, and between the church and our sisters and brothers in other Christian communities. If we have a realistic hope of universal salvation, then we need to live now as Christ's risen people, who hope and expect to spend the rest of eternity worshipping God with people from every culture, faith and social background in the world.

Notes:
1 *cf* Interchurch Group on Faith and Politics, *Breaking Down the Enmity*, Belfast: 1993, p. 88.
2 *Seeds of a new Church*, Dublin: Columba, 1994, pp 163-4.
3 Brian Lennon, *Two Church Marriages in Ireland: an ecclesiological problem*, University of Hull, MA thesis, 1979, p 69.
4 I am grateful to Rev Campbell Wilson for this story.

CHAPTER 8

The Church and society

The last chapter looked at some responses to the situation in Northern Ireland that Catholics might make as members of the church. In this chapter I want to look at responses that Catholics might make as members of society. I want to look at five areas: Catholics and politics, the priority of the Catholic Church in Northern Ireland, integrated education, the church and the issue of cultural identity, and the church and divorce. How much does our commitment to reconciliation and justice dominate what we do in these areas, or do we have other goals that are more important?

1. CATHOLICS AND POLITICS

The eucharist is a commemoration of Calvary. As such it remembers an event which came about in part because of the opposition of political and religious leaders to the message of Christ. That message was about reconciliation and justice. If our message today does not provoke opposition in both political and religious circles then, almost certainly, it has little to do with the message of Jesus of Nazareth. Those, then, who think that they can go to Mass for comfort and security and leave behind the turbulent world of political divisions are wrong.

In our preaching we need to accept the link between faith and social and political issues that the exodus story puts before us. The story is a rejection of any notion of a dualism that sees the spiritual as something dealing with a God who is not intrinsically involved in this world, and therefore sees questions arising from political issues as being outside the remit of Christian Churches. Ironically, the same attitude does not apply to issues of politics when they are connected with reproductive matters. The life of the unborn is often given more prominence in our church than the lives of the born.

However, we need to clarify immediately what is meant by the term 'politics'. Clearly churches have no role in party politics. But they have to be involved in politics in a wider sense. Part of the churches' work is to help to set a context in which politics is possible, that is, one in which there is sufficient consensus in society to allow democratic politics to function. Part of it is to do whatever it can to clarify the moral and ethical values that lie behind political decisions. The church also needs to throw its weight behind those who are more deprived in society.

We need to recognise that the way groups relate to each other in society is political in the broad sense. These relationships make an impact on the way we structure society and distribute money and other resources, and on the ideas that we have about one another. Thus, the fact that the Orange Order is an exclusively Protestant society makes an impact both on its members and on outsiders. In the same way, if all the organisations in a Catholic parish are made up only of Catholics, and do not have relationships with Protestants, this suggests to both Catholics and Protestants that the Catholic Church is in practice concerned only with Catholics. And, some will ask, why should it not be? The answer is because Catholics, in common with other Christians, want to be part of God's community.

The challenge of politics in the broad sense, and the need for Catholics to be involved in building just relationships in society, has been expressed time after time in the various social encyclicals of the church, most of which in practice receive little attention from Catholics as a whole.

There is a need for Catholics, out of their faith commitment, to contribute to a crucial task: helping to develop a Northern Ireland political identity. People often think of political identities as unchanging. This is not true. The identity of Protestant unionists in the south in 1925 had changed radically well before 1965. The republican identity of nationalists in the south changed deeply between 1916 and 1919, and again in response to the civil war. It also changed when De Valera brought Fianna Fáil into the Dáil in 1926, when the south was declared a republic in 1948, and the impact of the northern troubles has brought further change since 1969. The 1994 ceasefire represents an enormous change in the identity of republicans. Our question therefore should not be: do changes occur in political identity, but rather how can we best influence such change positively?

Whatever political settlement is arrived at in the future, the people living in what is now Northern Ireland will have to live with each other. In almost any political scenario Northern Ireland is going to continue as a political entity, albeit as part of some wider structure. There is therefore a crucial need to encourage anything that helps the development of a positive Northern Ireland identity for both nationalists and unionists. If all the churches in Northern Ireland gave themselves seriously to the task of encouraging such a process, it could make a dramatic impact for good. We could, for example, make this our primary task for the next decade.

There are three important questions to be addressed in this context: whom do we blame for creating our present problems? How useful is the idea of a nation state? And to what extent do nationalists want a withdrawal from Northern Ireland by the British government?

Whom do we blame?
A continuing theme in Irish nationalism is that the British have been responsible for grave injustice against the Irish. There is no doubt that successive British governments have committed grave injustices both in the way territory was seized in the island in the first instance, and in many of the actions carried out by governments since. But it should be remembered that Irish people were to the fore in every century – starting with Diarmuid McMurrough in the twelfth – in helping the British to achieve their aims. The North Cork Fusiliers, who put down the 1798 rebellion in Wexford, and who were mostly Irish, are one example among many.

The wrongs that the British have done to Irish people need to be acknowledged. This is crucial in the healing of memories. It applies to events such as the Ulster Plantations in the seventeenth and the Penal Laws in the eighteenth centuries. It also applies to the famine whose 150th anniversary falls in 1995. It also applies to more recent events such as Bloody Sunday and the unjustifiable killings that have been carried out by members of the security forces since 1968 and covered up. For the relatives of the victims of such killings there is a deep need that the truth about the killings be publicly admitted, and justice requires that their need be met. Further, it is impossible to build the sort of new relationships that are required within Ireland and Britain unless wrongs like these are admitted.

However, the fact that Britain was wrong to attempt to conquer Ireland in the first place does not tell us what action she is required to take now – apart from admitting guilt where appropriate. We do not now live in the twelfth, or the seventeenth or the nineteenth centuries.

Some argue that if a wrong was committed in the past then the only moral course is to undo this action, irrespective of what has happened in the meantime. But this assumes that wrong can always be undone in such a way as to restore the former situation. This is often simply not possible. An example is the destruction of native Indian lives, culture and property in America: can it be argued coherently that Manhattan island should be restored to the condition it was in before white people landed in America? Granted that the descendants of the original settlers have benefited from wrongs committed by their ancestors, does the work they have invested in the land count for nothing? Have they no rights?

The force of the argument is strengthened when one considers the practicality of restoring a previously existing situation.

Does this mean that the descendants of those who have committed oppression end up by being better off and at the same time having no moral guilt? This is quite a different question and it requires several distinctions. Yes, the descendants are better off. No, they are not guilty for what their ancestors did. Yes, they are bound to restore property to the rightful owners if the rightful owners can morally be established. This is almost never the case in nationalist disputes that have gone on for centuries. Apart from anything else there has been a certain amount of intermarriage since the seventeenth century, even in what is now Northern Ireland. Secondly, how does one prove ownership of property after 300 years? It is not possible. One might construct a case where clear lines of descent can be established. But how then does one assess the rights of the present occupiers and the rewards to which they are entitled for the improvements they have made to the land? Does that mean that those who benefited from land expropriation are therefore freed from all responsibility towards the descendants of those who suffered unjustly?

The answer is no, but we need to separate out two different meanings of the word 'responsibility'. In one sense 'responsibility' is associated with guilt. If I am responsible for robbing a person, then I am guilty of doing wrong and I should make recompense. But 'responsibility' has a second meaning and this has more to do with 'duty' than with 'guilt'. So, for example, German people born after World War Two bear no guilt for the holocaust. But that does not relieve them of all responsibility arising out of the holocaust. Precisely because a large proportion of Germans supported the Nazis who committed the holocaust, their descendants are in a different position in relation to Jewish people, than, for example, Australians would be. It is at the very least appropriate that a young German person would be deeply interested in the welfare of Jewish people because of the holocaust. One can go further and say that there is a duty on the German people as a whole, irrespective of their individual guilt, to work for the welfare of Jews.

In a similar way, one can speak of the responsibility of British people towards the Irish. Because of wrongs committed in the past, and wrongs in the area of justice that are still being maintained by the British government, British people have a particular duty to be concerned about the well-being of Irish people. However, this responsibility is not all one-sided. Irish people have also done great wrong to British people. The most obvious examples are the atrocities committed by the IRA. Most Irish people are not responsible for these atrocities and rejected the violence of the IRA. But the IRA are part of the Irish people, just as the Nazis were part of the German people. So it is at least appropriate that Irish people play a special role in seeking the welfare of British people as a result.

There are those who reject this line of reasoning on the grounds that they are individuals and as such have no connection with anything the IRA do, and therefore have no duty to their victims. This position only holds up as long as we can think of ourselves as isolated individuals. But once we see ourselves as members of a nation, a country, a class, or a club, once we pay taxes to a central government, once we pray as part of a Christian community, such individualism can no longer be maintained. We are then faced not only with our own sins and failings, but also with those of the groups to which we belong. Questions then emerge about group solidarity, group guilt, and a group's responsibility to make recompense for what some members of the group have done to others. In this context, the Irish and the British people have much work to do both for and with each other.

At the centre of this work will be the task of forgiveness, but also of repentance, of finding some way, as groups and as individuals, of acknowledging our own sins and those of our ancestors.

The idea of the nation state
A second theme in Irish nationalism, as we have seen, is that of the nation state. The category of nation state, however, is arguably one that does not lend itself to a solution of the northern conflict. Two nationalisms, each with their own definition of the state, are in conflict with each other: Irish and British. They differ in some respects. One element of the Irish version – to a greater or lesser extent – sees territorial integrity as central. British nationalism, in theory at least, is based on the consent of the governed. What this means is that England, Scotland, Wales and Northern Ireland are members of the UK by consent, or so it is claimed.[1]

The right to self-determination of a people has been increasingly recognised since the French Revolution, but asserting the right does not in itself answer all the problems. For one thing, it is notoriously difficult to decide what constitutes a people. Are the Northern Ireland unionists a people? Does one use the criterion of numbers to decide when a group is a people? If so, what territory does one use – the island of Ireland, Northern Ireland, or the British Isles? An argument can be made for each of these: Ireland, because it is an island, and because many believe the group living on the island constitute an ancient people; the British Isles because they were part of the same administration for almost 120 years; Northern Ireland because it has existed since 1920, because international laws recognise the boundaries established in Western Europe at the end of the Second World War, and because arguably this has also been recognised by the south in the Boundary Commission settlement in 1925 and *de facto* in the Anglo-Irish Agreement of 1985.

It is not only in Ireland that the limitations of nation states are becoming obvious. Much of modern government transcends the boundaries of nation states, and the trend in that direction is likely to increase, rather than decrease, both for economic and military reasons. Since the 1950s multi-national companies have gradually amassed greater power than that held by most governments in the world. This has led to the creation and the development of the EU, along with other international systems of government. Yet wider systems of government, such as the EU, have not succeeded in attracting the same emotional loyalty that nation states held in the past. At the same time, especially in the former Soviet Union, ethnic pride is leading minority groups to break away from the newly independent states that have arisen. Further, governments often get blamed for changes in social or moral values, or because they are no longer able to protect their countries from increased immigration that is a threat to indigenous jobs.

All this means that traditional notions of independence should be examined critically, especially in a situation of a double minority, each with their own history and strong feelings about identity, such as exists in Ireland. It also means that there is a growing and probably unstoppable thrust towards more international forms of government. But the task of winning legitimacy for these governments, and of enabling diverse and opposed groups to identify with them, is going to be complex and difficult.

Nicholas Colchester puts the dilemma well:

> Supranational government is needed but unwanted. Sub-national identity is wistfully desired, but is too often little

more than a costume parade. Nation-state government is still much desired but is being undressed, as it were, from above and below. Well-meaning internationalists talk interminably in smoke-filled rooms. Seething realists wish that conviction politics would return and show that this claimed need for a world order would vanish if only the older extroverts among the nation-states could walk tall again.[2]

In this context Colchester notes that the flag of Europe flies more in Scotland, Catalonia, Rhone-Alpes and Bavaria, than it does in London, Madrid, Paris and Berlin, 'precisely because it is a symbol of a counter-weight to those old, aloof capitals'.

A further problem with nation states is that of minorities. How does one cope with them? By re-partition? If not, how does one provide for their rights?

Throughout this century, especially through the influence of the UN, efforts have been made to protect minority rights and culture through laws made by the majority population and administered by them. This cannot happen unless two conditions are fulfilled: the majority population are convinced of the need for such laws, and there is sufficient trust between the two communities. In a real sense the minority are at the mercy of the majority. Neither of these conditions has so far been met within Northern Ireland. That is why nationalists – as part of a settlement – are insisting on a role for the Dublin government and also, though somewhat less clearly in recent years, on some form of power-sharing.

A second approach to catering for the rights of minorities is through a canton-like system, as in Switzerland. A solution based on power-sharing is therefore somewhat rare. Where it has been tried, as in Switzerland and in Belgium, it has been part of a system that also included federal or canton arrangements.

Irish nationalists face problems when the consequences of achieving a united Ireland are examined. Some of the difficulties that emerge are: the problem of control of the security forces, the likelihood of northern unionists having greater influence – and northern nationalists consequently less – in a united Ireland, and the fact that there are almost no circumstances in which unionists would consent to such a move.

However, behind criticism of Irish nationalism often lies an assumption: that the Irish should not only renounce their nationalism but replace it with British nationalism. The argument is never put as baldly as this but this is what is implied. If the Irish give up their claim to Northern Ireland without significant changes in British and Irish relationships, the result will be that British nationalism will simply replace the Irish variety. For those who support this view, British nationalism is generally assumed to be superior to the Irish version, which is often described as tribalism. Because the argument is never worked out the assumption is never exposed and tested. Irish political thinking is seen as being on the same level as African or Central American tribes, whose politics are implicitly seen as being vastly inferior to the enlightened politics of Britain.

In fact it is arguable that Irish political thinking is marginally ahead of Britain's (the Forum for a New Ireland was a significant sign of change) and that both are well behind that of some tribal systems. Where the Irish have been ahead has been in their willingness to think in terms of some joint approach to the problem: the initiative for the Anglo-Irish Agreement came from the Irish.

The consequences of British withdrawal

Part of traditional nationalism has been the desire for the political separation of the whole island of Ireland from the UK and its unification as a separate unified state. Apart from difficulties with the idea of independent states in an increasingly interdependent world, there are also other issues raised when we examine this aim.

One is that it is not clear what proportion of nationalists in Northern Ireland want British withdrawal. While one needs to be cautious about opinion polls, nonetheless it is significant that only 32% of Catholics in Northern Ireland opted for a united Ireland as their first choice in a 1993 poll.[3] This is why it is at least arguable that when people say they want a united Ireland what they are saying is in practice something negative and not positive: they want an end to domination by unionists and the British. This is a perfectly reasonable demand and one could also think of a variety of ways in which it could be met, e.g. by changes in symbols, control of policing, job distribution, north-south structures, etc. It is no coincidence that these were the main items in the negotiations taking place between the two governments and the political parties within Northern Ireland in 1993-1994. It is quite a different agenda from trying to work out the political structures on the island in the event of a British withdrawal.

Secondly, constitutionally it would be well-nigh impossible for the Westminster parliament to expel Northern Ireland from the UK against the will of the majority. What argument could they put to oppose those in Scotland who want independence? Given the quite tenuous links that hold the UK together it would not be in the inter-

THE CHURCH AND SOCIETY

est of anyone concerned about its preservation to see Northern
Ireland expelled from it.

Does this discussion lead us to conclude that Irish nationalism
has no validity, that it has no right to pursue its goal of territorial
integrity? No. Irish nationalists have as much right as British
nationalists to pursue their goals. However, the above analysis suggests that any Irish nationalism that is based primarily on territory
is not going to help to resolve the northern conflict. The rationale
for this is that there is no way that it can take account of the fact that
there are two minorities on the island: nationalists within Northern
Ireland and unionists within the context of the island as a whole.
Ireland is not unique in facing this problem. Similar issues arise
elsewhere, especially in Eastern Europe after the collapse of the
Soviet Union. In each case crude statism is unhelpful.

This discussion has shown that a concept of self-determination
that does not deal adequately with the identity of other groups is
inadequate to deal with the complexity of relationships that exist on
the islands of Ireland and Britain. These points have been accepted
by both governments and by the SDLP. However they have not yet
found political structures to enshrine a new, more inclusive vision.
Nor have these views been accepted by everyone in Northern
Ireland, or in the Republic. If they were conceded, and if it was also
conceded that unionism on its own has similar flaws, we would be
a long way on the road to a lasting peace. We would have started on
the path of reconciliation by admitting that all the different political
groups need to look together for new structures within which we
can do politics.

2. THE PRIORITY OF THE CATHOLIC CHURCH IN NORTHERN IRELAND

A second issue that needs to be addressed under the heading of
Catholics and society is: what is the actual, as distinct from the theor-
etical, priority of Catholics? The answer of many in Northern
Ireland is: Mass and sacraments. But next to this many will put
education because they see it as the way for more deprived people
to rise into the middle classes.

The aim of creating a strong educated middle-class Catholic
group in Northern Ireland has some attractions. Grammar schools,
or secondary schools with a good A-Level record, can be an opportunity for Catholics to get university or other qualifications, which
in turn can lead to professional well-paid jobs. Indeed, one of the
major changes in Northern Ireland is that such opportunities are
now more available to Catholics than used be the case (although

Catholics remain 2.2 times as likely to be unemployed as Protestants).
Entry to the middle class can often reduce the terrible suffering that
can go with multiple deprivation, such as a higher record of hospi-
tal admissions, of mental illness, of deaths from violence, etc.
Further, it is natural and appropriate that any group would work
for its own improvement. But what of those who get left behind?
What consideration is given to their needs? Again we have to ask,
who is the community? Are deprived people at the centre of the
Catholic community in practice? If not, can we say that we are in
fact in touch with Christ?

The issue, then, is not simply one of material advance. We also
have to ask who are we including and who we are excluding. We
can be falsely idealistic in responding to this by saying that we are
including everyone. That is never true. We need to be honest about
naming those who are being excluded and then facing up to our
responsibilities to them. What this means is that we can never claim
to have completed the task of building a Christian community.
Each advance in rights for some exposes other situations and
groups whose rights are neglected.

3. Integrated Education

One of the aspects most commonly seized on by newcomers to the
Northern conflict is integrated education. In the north the two
divided communities are often ignorant of each other's perceptions,
and children grow up separated from each other. In this context the
most obvious solution seems to be to educate them together. This
view is not only held by outsiders who are new to the conflict but
by others who have a long history of working realistically for reconciliation and justice. However, some of those opposed to integrated
education can also claim such credentials. It should not be assumed
that Catholic priests are always on the side of segregated education.
In a postal survey of priests in 1986, Gerald McElroy found that
while 53% were opposed in principle to integrated education,
40.9% were not. However the overall response rate was only 36.9%,
and in Down and Connor, the largest diocese, it was only 21%.[4]

The onus is certainly on those opposed to integrated education
to show how segregated schools contribute to community relations.
Some argue that only in a school under Catholic control will a child
be given the full Catholic ethos that comes from parents, relatives
and school all trying to inculcate the same values. There is no doubt
that Catholic schools are one of the elements that go to make up the
Catholic identity in Northern Ireland. This is a strong identity and

in a world where local identities are under constant threat this is an important value. The danger of such an identity, however, is precisely that it is a separate identity. In Northern Ireland that tends to reinforce sectarianism. This is not a necessary outcome, but those who support separate education need to show that they are supplying the necessary balance by ensuring that there is a strong cross-community programme in the school. By 'strong' I mean something far greater than one or two cross-community meetings a term. It needs to be a regular and on-going programme. In 1994 just over one third of schools in Northern Ireland were involved in the government-run cross-community contact scheme.

The case of those opposed to integrated education is at times greatly weakened by what looks like sectarianism. An example is insisting that children from integrated schools receive First Communion at a different time from those in Catholic schools. Sometimes children from integrated schools are also required to attend extra religious classes on the sometimes dubious pretext that they have not been prepared as well as the children in Catholic schools. Part of the problem in assessing these issues is that there may well be integrated schools – just as there are Catholic schools – where preparation is less than adequate. But in that case Catholic priests should visit integrated schools to find out if in fact the children are any less well prepared.

However, those who support integrated education have themselves questions to answer: to what extent are such schools really integrated? In the early days of setting up integrated schools there can be a tremendous experience of learning about each other's traditions and developing the trust to tackle serious questions with each other. But as the school gets established that dynamic element can run down. Such schools need to look at their level of creative conflict. If, for example, there is no conflict about community relations then one can question whether the school is going in the right direction.

4. The Church and Cultural Identity

The Catholic Church in Northern Ireland has often been accused of being over-identified with Irish culture. This charge is based on clerical involvement in and support for the Gaelic Athletic Association, which controls Gaelic football and hurling, and the Irish language. The charge is part of a wider claim that the 'churches are chaplains to the two tribes'. The assumption behind the charge is that churches should support greater pluralism. There is also a specific charge against the GAA: that the rule by which it bans members of the security forces from joining the organisation shows that it is a political, and not simply a sporting organisation. It has no similar rule against nationalist paramilitaries joining.

As an institution, the power and influence of the Catholic Church have been linked with the rise of Catholics as a whole on the island for the past two hundred years. That rise has in turn been linked with nationalism, of various hues, since 1798. Almost all Catholic priests are Irish in national identity. Having gone to Catholic schools and played Gaelic games it is as natural for them to be associated with the GAA, as it is for many better-off Protestants to be members of the Irish Rugby Football Union. Both Catholics and Protestants play soccer. However, very few northern Catholics play rugby and almost no Protestants play Gaelic. It would therefore help if more Catholics schools played rugby, and more Protestant schools started playing Gaelic. Both are good games. It does not help community relations in Northern Ireland for either to be associated exclusively with one community. It is a sign of the great lack of self-confidence that exists in each community that neither is willing to play the other's game to any great extent.

One reaction to this suggestion is to say that it is typical of the unrealistic nature of ecumenical theological reflection on Northern Ireland. Given the context, so the argument goes, it is simply not possible for Catholic schools to play rugby or vice versa for Protestant schools in relation to Gaelic. But the reality is that nothing changes in Northern Ireland until someone starts doing something surprising. Perhaps games are not the place to start. But if not, where should one start? Once again we come back to our basic question: what is the priority for the Christian community in Northern Ireland: is it reconciliation with justice, or is it the maintenance of separate communities?

The GAA's rule excluding members of the security forces should be changed. It is an historical anomaly. Doing so will make little practical difference. The security forces are not rushing to join. But it will remove another irritant from the situation. Failing to do so leaves the GAA open to the charge of being politically sectarian on the basis that it excludes the security forces, but it did not exclude nationalist paramilitaries.[5]

As regards the Irish language, in reality few priests show much enthusiasm for it. It is one of many threatened minority languages in Europe. As such it deserves all the support it can get. At the moment there is a resurgence of interest in the language. This interest is shown in the number of kindergarten and primary schools started by lay people, without state assistance, that teach through the medium of Irish, both in Northern Ireland and in the Republic.

Finally, the Catholic Church needs to show proper respect for the identity of British people in Northern Ireland. Doing this does not necessarily involve what many British/unionists want: to have Irish nationalists accept a dominant position for British culture. But part of the task of healing is that both sides in the north develop an appreciation that there is good in each side, as well as being critical of what is bad. We have no problem doing the latter. We have plenty with the former.

5. THE CHURCH AND DIVORCE

The Catholic bishops' position is that divorce is wrong. However, the arguments that they use to support the banning of divorce by state law are primarily sociological, not theological. At the 1974 Forum debate, they pointed to the experience of other countries where divorce has been introduced where it has always led to a steep increase in the number of families breaking up. Since keeping the family together is an important value for Catholics and since the majority of people in the Republic are Catholic, they argued that there should be no change in the law. They accepted that Catholics could legitimately disagree with them.

In many ways this debate exposed the weakness of the bishops' position. As the number of people who wanted divorce in the south increased throughout the 1980s, so the inevitability of its introduction became more apparent. In 1993 Pope Paul II, while visiting Africa, reminded Muslim leaders that Islamic law should only be applied to Muslim faithful, and not to countries where Muslims had a majority. The same argument could be applied in Ireland.[6]

However, the bishops also exposed some of the weaknesses in the position of their more liberal interrogators, particularly in relation to pluralism. As they pointed out, citing pluralism was not in itself an adequate argument for minority rights, because there had to be limits which arose from the common good, the objective moral order, and the confines of a proper civilisation. Thus even if a majority agreed with the Jehovah Witnesses' position on blood transfusion it would still be wrong to support this in law. In other words, arguing for the need for pluralism simply begs the question of where to draw the line between public and private morality and why.[7]

The debate at the 1974 Forum also showed the problem of using 'rights' language. At times the bishops seemed to accept that divorce is a right, which makes it difficult to see how it is not a right for everyone, north and south. But even if it is a right, it has to be balanced against other rights, such as those of children.

The constitutional ban on divorce has frequently been used by unionists, not unreasonably in the view of some southern politicians, as evidence of church control of the south. This made the possibility of a united Ireland more remote. To this the bishops reply that changing the ban on divorce would not make the south any more attractive to unionists in terms of a united Ireland, because the unionist opposition to it was unconditional. Those people who wanted divorce to be legalised were therefore asking the bishops to support something that was going to do great harm to the family's place in society. At the same time it was not going to achieve anything positive for those who wanted a united Ireland.

But the bishops' view that a change in divorce law would make no impact on the northern conflict was questionable. A major element in the conflict are the fears that exist in the unionist/Protestant community. An important part of these is fear of the Catholic Church. Many Protestants see the Roman Church as a very large, monolithic structure. Anyone who knows the church from the inside may be somewhat bemused at this description, given the divisions that exist. But that is the way that a large proportion of Protestants see it. And, in this instance, their perception is very influential.

The issue of divorce was still very much alive in 1994 because the coalition government, this time between Fianna Fáil and Labour, were committed to changing the constitutional ban. The fact that Fianna Fáil were committed to it, although in a luke warm way in much of the party, suggested that change was likely. But the government's plans ran into legal difficulties when their proposals for the settlement of property after divorce were found unconstitutional by the Supreme Court. The new coalition, between Fine Gael, Labour and Democratic Left, which came into office in December 1994, remained committed to divorce reform.

Notes:

1 Arthur Aughey in *Under siege: Ulster Unionism and the Anglo-Irish Agreement*, Belfast: Blackstaff, 1989, gives one of the more coherent accounts of unionism.

2 *cf* Nicholas Colchester, 'Goodbye, Nation-State. Hello … What?', *The New York Times*, 17 July 1994.

3 Irish Times\Coopers and Lybrand poll, *The Irish Times*, 3 December 1993.
4 *The Catholic Church and the Northern Ireland Crisis, 1968-1986*, Dublin: Gill and Macmillan, 1991.
5 *cf* Seamus Murphy SJ, 'I don't support the IRA, but …', *Studies*, Vol 82, No 327, Autumn 1993, p 281.
6 *The Irish Times*, 4 Feb 1993, p 7: 'Pope criticises Muslim states as tour begins.'
7 For excellent discussions of this and other church-state issues *cf* Vincent MacNamara, *The Truth in Love: Reflections on Christian Morality*, Dublin: Gill and Macmillan, 1988 and Patrick Hannon, *Church, State, Morality and Law*, Dublin: Gill and Macmillan, 1992.

CHAPTER 9

Constitutional and political suggestions

In the light of the political realities that we have discussed in our earlier chapters, and of the faith elements that we outlined when we looked at who the Christian God is, what sort of constitutional and political structures should be set within Northern Ireland, and between Britain and Ireland?

The answer to this question needs to be dealt with at several levels: the constitutional status of Northern Ireland; political structures within Northern Ireland; and the role of the Dublin government within Northern Ireland. A settlement that allows one or other side to dominate would neither be reconciling nor just. What kind of compromises should be made, and what sort of compromises might be politically possible?

Readers may well disagree with the suggestions made. That in itself is not important. What matters is that we ask ourselves how well these suggestions fit in with what we have seen in the scriptures. Where we think they do not, can we come up with other more appropriate suggestions? There is plenty of room for a variety of answers. But not all answers will work: British only, or Irish only answers are not in keeping with the scriptures.

In the scriptures, as we have seen, reconciliation is central. This is because the very nature of God is centred in relationships: relationships between the three divine Persons, between God and us, and between human communities. If we were to summarise the divine project, as we have outlined it, in two words they would be: 'building community'. Central to that task is the restoring of community where it has broken down. But, equally, community can only exist where there is justice or right relationships. All of this raises issues of forgiveness for hurt that has occurred in the past, of taking others seriously and attempting to understand their pain as well as our own, and of finding the right way to handle conflict.

At a constitutional level, northern nationalists and the people of the Republic need to recognise formally and legally that Northern

Ireland shall remain part of the UK as long as a major
ple wish. There is also a need for either a Bill of Righ
domesticate European and UN human rights legislatior

Secondly, within Northern Ireland there needs to b ___wer-
sharing executive with extensive powers, with a built in cost for
failure to agree.

Thirdly, new north-south cooperative structures are needed in
the areas of trade, tourism, legal matters and negotiations with the
EU.

Fourthly, consideration should be given to joint north-south
approaches to the EU.

Fifthly, radical changes need to be made in policing in order to
make the security forces properly accountable, and to ensure that
they reflect the British and Irish identities of the people of Northern
Ireland.

Each of these points needs to be elaborated briefly, in the light of
the political realities that have been discussed, and of the outline of
the values we find in the scriptures. I will consider the first four in
this chapter and policing in the next.

1. CONSTITUTIONAL ISSUES

One of the points made in this book is that the relationship between
the British and Irish governments is crucial to the whole conflict
because it sets the context within which the communities in
Northern Ireland have to relate to each other. The fact that there has
been a comparatively good relationship between the two governments is one of the reasons why the conflict has been more limited
than in other parts of the world. But the ambiguities that exist
between the governments have also been the source of both false
fears and false hopes within the northern communities. The Downing Street Declaration went a long way to clarifying the inter-gov-
ernmental relationship, particularly in the area of self-determination. At a constitutional level it confirmed what was obvious: that
there could be no change in Northern Ireland's position as part of
the UK without majority consent. But it left the issue of Articles
Two and Three still to be dealt with as part of on-going negotiations.

Articles Two and Three
The key concession that nationalists should make constitutionally
as well as *de facto* is to recognise that Northern Ireland shall remain
part of the UK as long as the majority of its people so wish. One pos-

sible way of doing this would be to distinguish between the territory of the nation and that of the state. (The text of the Articles is given on page 32.)

The essential difficulty with retaining Article Two is that it includes both an assumption and a legal claim that the state of Ireland should be contiguous with the nation as it has defined it. If the Article expressed the belief of the Irish people that the territory of the nation includes Northern Ireland, but confined the territory of the state to what is now the Republic of Ireland, and further expressed the aspiration that the territory of the nation and the state would some day coincide, then it would be coherent with the principle of consent contained in the Downing Street Declaration. As it stands it is not.

What this change would mean is that the Irish people would give up the claim to have the right to enact laws for Northern Ireland. (Article Three currently does not give up this right. It merely says that the laws of the southern parliament *de facto* shall not apply to Northern Ireland).

As things stand, the Irish government has no effective means of imposing its laws on Northern Ireland. It has accepted that unity can only come about by consent. The only difference, then, made by changing the constitution in the way suggested is that the south would give up a right that cannot be proved philosophically – although equally it cannot be disproved – and which cannot be implemented politically.

Would the change make any difference to Ireland's position vis-à-vis Northern Ireland in international law? It is difficult to see how it could. The burden of international law is against the Irish claim, since such law has a strong bias to accept European boundaries as established since World War II. (Former Yugoslavia is the only example of changed boundaries in Western Europe and those changes were brought about in the face of the opposition of international law and morality).

Changing Article Two and deleting Article Three would benefit the Irish people because it would make the constitution coherent. It would keep intact the definition of the Irish nation as – probably – the vast majority want it. It would also give support to the policy of unity only by consent. It would recognise that such consent is not at present forthcoming. But it would not preclude unity in the future.

When these arguments are put to northern nationalists many respond by opposing them on the grounds that they will never give up their nationality. However, changing Articles Two and Three should not mean a change in nationality for northerners. The nation in the proposed definition would include everyone born on the island of Ireland who chooses to be Irish. The definition also states the belief of the Irish people that the nation – as distinct from the state – includes the territory of the whole island. Without such a statement there might be arguments as to whether the city of Armagh, for example, would be seen by the Irish Constitution as British or Irish.

Whatever formula were chosen it would be essential that the national, citizen and residency needs of northerners to be Irish were recognised to the full. It would also be vital that the British government continue to affirm the right of people in Northern Ireland to choose dual Irish and British nationality and citizenship. Further, the status of Northern Ireland should be defined in a British Act of Parliament along the lines of the preamble to the Anglo-Irish Agreement. This emphasises the unique relationship between the two countries and the need to work to reconcile and recognise both the British and Irish traditions that exist in Northern Ireland. It would help if the Dáil mirrored this with an Act of its own.

In the south, the church could enter more seriously into the debate around Articles Two and Three of the constitution. By this I do not mean that the church should recommend one particular stance. But people should be asked, in the light of the scriptures, to examine their motivation for retaining these Articles and to see if there are any hidden elements of imperialism in it. On the other hand, those who want to cut Northern Ireland off and ignore it should be asked to look at their own anger and sense of powerlessness. Those who stress the rights of unionists alone, or of nationalists alone, should be asked how this builds community in accordance with what God wants of us. By raising questions like these the church could make an important contribution to creating a situation in which politics would be possible.

A Bill of Rights?
The second constitutional change that is needed is a Bill of Rights. This view is supported by all the Northern Ireland political parties. Opposition to it has come from the British government which is anxious to avoid a situation where the power of the government would be limited. Americans, in particular, find the lack of a written constitution extraordinary and they are right. There have been many problems over the years with the constitution in the Republic but its importance in the protection and development of human rights, slow though progress is, has been immense.

The easiest measure would be to domesticate European and UN human legislation. The effect of this would be to allow citizens of the UK to have the protection of this legislation within the UK, instead of having to go through long drawn out and expensive legal procedures in international fora. It would also be an interesting, and possibly immensely constructive exercise, to see if Northern Ireland political parties could draw up a constitution for the region. As part of such an exercise, political parties should be asked to draw up principles on divisive issues such as marches, and flags and emblems. These principles should emphasise two points: a) that people have a right to express their identity; and b) that the symbols of a group should never be flaunted in a way that offends other groups.

Changing Articles Two and Three and bringing in a Bill of Rights would be powerful elements in any strategy based on reconciliation and justice. Each side would be taking the other seriously. Neither side would get what it wants completely.

2. NORTHERN IRELAND POLITICAL STRUCTURES

The second change which is needed is to set up a power-sharing executive within Northern Ireland with extensive powers over almost all areas of government and this should be insisted on by nationalists in return for constitutional concessions.

At first sight this may not seem a problem. It is built into the Anglo-Irish Agreement that if there is cross-community support for devolving any areas of government to a Northern Ireland assembly, then that should be done.

However, the difficulty is that pious aspirations to set up a power-sharing executive will not necessarily deliver one.

To make power-sharing work it may be necessary to build in a cost factor for failure to agree on a certain proportion of proposals. This could be achieved by the British government insisting that all Northern Ireland budgets will be passed by – for example – 70% of those attending the power-sharing executive. (If political parties refuse to attend then those who attend should be able to pass both legislation and budgets.) If the executive fails to agree then the responsibility for dealing with legislation will pass to the Secretary of State. However, such referrals will delay the passage of legislation considerably. The British government should also then reduce the relevant budget.

This proposal would allow Northern Ireland parties the right to refuse to pass legislation, but for the first time a direct cost for such refusals would be built in which would come into play as soon as such a refusal became apparent. This is the reverse of the present situation where the supporters of Northern Ireland political parties face no direct cost for refusing to share power. It should be noted that EU countries, despite often deep economic differences, manage to agree on community budgets because failure to do so would be too costly, economically and politically.

The British government, with the agreement of the Irish government, could set up such a structure, even if negotiations between the political parties do not lead to agreement.

Of course there are problems with the idea of power-sharing. If we ever get beyond sectarian head counting in Northern Ireland, how will we get out of structures which are sectarian based? A second problem is the likelihood that a power-sharing executive will willy-nilly encourage greater departmental rivalry within the government and civil service than would otherwise be the case. But the answer to these and other objections is to face the fact that we have at the moment a divided community. If we are to avoid one community dominating the other then we need to have a power-sharing structure. It will be time enough to deal with the problem of getting rid of such structures when they are no longer necessary.

3. NORTH-SOUTH STRUCTURES

A third element in any settlement is the need for north-south structures within Ireland. These have been proposed at different times by both Albert Reynolds as Taoiseach, and Patrick Mayhew as Secretary of State. Unionists were also open to some north-south structures during the 1990-92 talks.

The Irish government insisted that new north-south structures should have executive, and not merely consultative, powers.

Clearly the Dáil would be the source of authority on the southern side for any such structures. On the northern side there are two possible sources of their authority. One is a new devolved assembly. In principle unionists should have no objection if this were the case, because in any power-sharing assembly they would have a veto. The British government could of course set up north-south structures without the consent of the unionists, if they wished, by making the Westminster parliament the source of their authority. However, by November 1994 there was no indication that they were open to this possibility.

At the opening of the Forum for Peace and Reconciliation, in October 1994, Albert Reynolds mentioned the following as areas

which could be covered by cross-border structures: 'inward investment, tourism, many elements of agriculture and fisheries, a clean
and pure environment, energy and communications'.[1] The island
as a whole could benefit immensely from joint north-south co-operation in any of these areas.

There have also been proposals for joint legal structures. In 1973
the British Prime Minister, as part of the Sunningdale negotiations,
accepted the idea of a common law-enforcement area. This was
designed to overcome difficulties about extradition. However, during
the negotiations leading to the Anglo-Irish Agreement the proposal
to set up joint north-south courts met with determined opposition
from unionists in the Northern Ireland judiciary, chiefly Lord
Justice Lowry, and the British refused to make the proposal part of
the Agreement. This was a pity because there would be obvious
benefits from a security point of view. Undoubtedly there would be
legal difficulties in interpreting the law of two different regions. But
because Irish law is closely modelled on British law these would be
much less than those faced by, for example, the European Courts of
Justice in interpreting laws of countries with very different legal
systems. In any future settlement it is important that the issue of
mixed courts be faced.

The issue of north-south structures, like many in the northern
conflict, has implications both at the level of identity and at a practical level. For unionists, such structures represent the threat of at
least partial rule by a Dublin government. Since the main purpose
of unionism is to avoid such rule, their reaction is understandable.
But it also anachronistic. It is a reaction based on the assumption
that any member of the European Union still has complete sovereignty, which is not the reality. Behind unionist rejection of north-
south links lies the constant fear that if they accept them it will be a
step in the direction of a united Ireland.

For nationalists, often for exactly opposite reasons, north-south
structures are also an identity issue. Some see such structures in
precisely the same way as unionists, that is a step towards a united
Ireland. Others see them as a partial recognition that Northern
Ireland is not simply British, but both Irish and British in its identity.

However, arguments over identity, of their very nature, tend to
be irrational. Just as unionist opposition to north-south structures is
anachronistic, so nationalist enthusiasm for them – or for the particular structures under discussion – can be puzzling. Thus it is hard
to see why so much fuss is made by either side over a proposal to
have an all-Ireland Tourist Board, to take one example. This seems

to reduce large-scale and solemn issues like self-determination to the level of struggles over the control of the allocation of bed and breakfast accommodation. This particular discussion would be much more comprehensible if it were about more serious and difficult issues, such as joint legal structures, or the most difficult issue of all, an all-Ireland Police Authority.

4. A JOINT APPROACH TO THE EU

A fourth element is joint north-south approaches to the EU. The argument for this is that it would fit in with the growing EU emphasis on regions, and that it would be more effective for both north and south to lobby together since they have common interests.

However, there are difficulties. For one thing, EU regions are not firmly established and there is no agreement that they should transcend state borders. Secondly, it is highly unlikely that the EU is going to allow structures to develop that would enable regions to be directly represented. This would dilute the power of the states upon which the EU is currently based, and it would require very many more units to be represented at Brussels since the number of possible regions could be very great.

It might be possible to overcome some of these difficulties by accepting that on occasion, or in relation to particular issues, the Belfast-based power-sharing executive would agree that the Dublin rather than the British government would represent its interests. This would be economically attractive, for example, to northern farmers. But the British government, whose agricultural interests do not coincide with those of Northern Ireland, would have to agree to such a change. They might well do so, if it were part of a wider package that showed signs of leading to a lasting peace.

One could think of a further possibility: that the Irish government would be willing to share its EU representation on some issues with Northern Ireland.[2] This would be in keeping with the Republic's stated commitment to unity. However, any such suggestion would face opposition from southern political interests, whose willingness to make sacrifices for the development of good relationships with the north would be tested.

I want now to turn to the most difficult issue of all in the northern conflict: policing.

Notes:
1 Speech at opening of Forum, 28 October 1994.
2 This was suggested by Garret FitzGerald in *The Irish Times* in October 1994.

CHAPTER 10

Policing

The issue of security is particularly painful for northern nationalists because it is at this point that many feel the conflict most deeply.

Much of the issue of policing has to do with practical questions about what kind of structures are best. This often involves choices between different good ways of proceeding which means it is perfectly appropriate for Christians to disagree. Where the gospels can provide a particular challenge is in looking at the sum total of the positions taken by a group and subjecting them to searching questions. So, if at the conclusion of our discussion we have reached a position where nationalists have no responsibility to do anything about policing in practice, then there are grounds for suspecting that we have not taken the unionist community seriously and therefore have not been inspired by Christ's example of making peace with his enemies. (Protestants and unionists face exactly the same challenge when they propose all-unionist or all-British solutions to the conflict).

Security is seen by nationalists as an issue of justice – people have a right to be treated with respect by the security forces – and of identity – the present security forces represent and act on behalf of the British state.

Principles governing good policing
In 1979 the UN adopted a Code of Conduct for Law Enforcement Officials.[1] One of its first points was on the issue of representation.

In the theory of Western democratic society, the police should act on behalf of the state which represents the people through the government which is elected by the people. In practice, naturally enough, things are not that simple. For one thing, governments seldom represent deprived people. The story of the twentieth century in Western Europe has in part been the success of the struggle against poverty by the majority of people, who are at least comparatively rich. That means that the poor have less political influence. They are a minority and often badly organised. But no matter how much they organise they will never have the influence of a majority or of the wealthy. So when we say that the state represents the people it is important to remember that deprived people are only included in this statement to a very limited extent.

This is particularly true of policing. The largest crimes, and those that often attract the lowest sentences, are white collar crimes. The Beef Tribunal in the south in 1992-93, which cost between £25m and £35m, was a classic example of this. In the Republic no one spent time in prison for tax evasion between the foundation of the state and 1986.[2] However, many crimes are also committed by deprived people. Unemployed people often feel useless and angry. This is not surprising, given the status that society puts on having a job, and given that employment is one of the key ways in which wealth is distributed. Bored and angry people who feel useless are more likely to commit crime. The job of the police is to prevent crime and to arrest law breakers. So it is not surprising that there is often conflict between deprived people and the police and that police are often seen by deprived people as protecting the better off.

Of course a great proportion of crime is also committed by deprived people against deprived people. This is particularly so in Northern Ireland where working class areas suffered far more than the leafy suburbs from paramilitary crime. Very often the suffering was imposed by paramilitaries supposedly from their own side.

In Northern Ireland this standard source of conflict is magnified in nationalist areas because many people see themselves as Irish and the police as British. The normal consensus required for proper policing, even in a class-divided society, does not therefore exist. The argument, then, that the police are the arm of the state which represents the people cannot be sustained uncritically in Northern Ireland. It is imperative that we move to a situation where there is agreement about policing in order to make proper representation possible.

The UN Code of Conduct insists that as well as being representative a police force should also be responsive and accountable to the community as a whole, and that it should have an independent mechanism for complaints. How can these principles be implemented in Northern Ireland?

I want to look firstly at accountability, local liaison groups, and identity. Secondly, I will suggest changes that might help the situation.

1. The current situation

Accountability

In the first instance the police are accountable to the law. This is the crucial difference between a police state and one that is properly democratic. But it is only of relevance where the law is just, where the police either keep the law or are punished for failing to do so, and where this can be seen to be the case. It would be difficult to show that these conditions are met satisfactorily in Northern Ireland. There is no written constitution in the UK. This means that the will of parliament is supreme. In practice governments are restrained to a certain extent firstly by some important legislation of previous parliaments which can take on some of the hallmarks of constitutional legislation, and secondly by international conventions into which the British Government has entered, such as the UN Charter, the two UN Covenants on Human Rights, the European Convention on Human Rights and Fundamental Freedoms, and the European Social Charter. However, none of these international conventions apply directly to UK law unless specifically adopted by parliament. To avail of their rights under the conventions, UK citizens have to seek redress either through the appropriate European or international structures. Naturally such legal procedures are expensive and slow.

What this means is that policing – in Northern Ireland and elsewhere in the UK – is subject only to the crudities of laws enacted by majority rule in parliament without sufficient protection from international conventions. A further problem, not unique to Northern Ireland, is the difficulty in challenging the credibility of security personnel in court. In Northern Ireland only four members of the British army were convicted of murder committed while on duty, despite the fact that approximately 350 people have been killed by security force members while on duty, many in disputed circumstances. One of the soldiers convicted – Private Thain – was released after serving less than three years of a life sentence and reinstated in the army. This shows in a startling manner the lengths to which British authorities were prepared to go to protect the security forces.

Equally startling is the Stalker case, where at the very least a *prima facie* case of conspiracy to pervert the course of justice was found to exist by John Stalker, but where the Northern Ireland DPP, under instructions from the Attorney General, decided that no case should be prosecuted.

Also, there is strong evidence that British army and RUC intelligence personnel handled agents within both nationalist and loyalist paramilitary organisations in cases where these agents may have participated in conspiracy to murder. The Nelson case has been perhaps the worst example of this.[3]

It is also remarkable that compensation has been given by the government to victims of transgressions by the security forces in so many cases, and that so few of the perpetrators of these crimes have been found guilty by the courts.

Given the limited availability of constitutional rights, the delays in getting redress through international fora, and the few convictions of security force members, it is not surprising that many people lack confidence in the system of justice in Northern Ireland. But there are other mechanisms of accountability: the Police Authority, the police complaints procedure and others introduced by Sir Patrick Mayhew as Secretary of State in June 1992. The Police Authority is appointed by the Secretary of State. It is meant to be a body representative of the community as a whole to which 'the wishes and fears of the community on policing' can be expressed.[4] Up to 1994 its membership was kept secret because of the legitimate fear of attack by paramilitaries, although in theory it is as far as practicable representative of the whole community. Its powers are limited. It determines the size of the RUC. It provides and maintains all buildings, equipment and supplies for the police. It appoints senior officers. It can require the Chief Constable to submit reports on certain matters and comment on what he produces. But it cannot require him to act differently in the future. It acts as the complaints and discipline authority for senior officers and keeps itself informed about the way in which complaints against lower ranks are handled. It maintains financial and budgetary control of expenditure on the police service. While it is entitled to decide on policy issues, it has power only over policy and not over operational issues. Crucially, it is the Chief Constable, and not the Police Authority, who decides what constitutes policy and what is deemed operational. Nationalist political parties have refused to nominate members because they believe the powers of the Authority are too limited.

The Police Authority itself has criticised the legislation governing it, and the limits on its powers. Some of the points it made in 1993 were: that parliament failed to delineate clearly the different responsibilities of the three main agencies or officers governing policing: the Secretary of State, the Police Authority and the Chief Constable. This has undermined agreements negotiated between the Authority and the RUC. Secondly, and related to this, while the

Authority has control over police budgets, important elements of spending are subject to central government control. Thirdly, the Authority has no power over the way in which police resources are deployed. Fourthly, there is no legal obligation on a Chief Constable to follow the Authority's advice. Nor are there meaning-ful sanctions, short of dismissal, that the Authority can employ against a Chief Constable who refuses to act on its advice. This means that the Authority can only influence RUC policies and stand-ards to a very limited extent. Fifthly, 'the Authority is responsible for making arrangements to obtain the views of local people about policing but is unable to ensure that those views are reflected in the strategic direction of the RUC.'[5] Sixthly, they find a conflict between the Authority's responsibility to act as a body through which the police should be accountable to the community and its responsibility to provide the police with support services.

In 1992 the Secretary of State, Patrick Mayhew, announced some changes in policing. He intended to appoint an independent com-missioner for RUC holding centres; to create the post of indepen-dent assessor of military complaints procedures; to issue a draft code of practice governing the treatment of people detained under the Prevention of Terrorism Act; and to introduce a scheme to mon-itor and reduce the time which prisoners spend in custody on remand. These were welcome changes, but they go nowhere near the sort of accountability that would exist if the Police Authority were given satisfactory powers.

Suggestions for changes in the Police Authority will be made below.

Police Community liaison
Some argue that an element of accountability is given by police community liaison committees. Several of these have operated throughout Northern Ireland. Some were formal groups based on District Councils, or groups who saw such liaison as part of their task, like the Derry Peace and Reconciliation Group. Others, like the Drumcree Faith and Justice Group in Portadown, did a lot of liaison work, but refused to accept the formal appellation because they opposed the RUC's policy of putting Orange marches though nationalist areas in the town. Liaison was often effectively carried out in private by individuals – sometimes priests.

What impact has such liaison had?

In a report in 1992 Ronald Weitzer found that formal committees were dominated by unionists and were deferential to the RUC.

Only three of seventeen committees were chaired by non-unionists, six had no Catholics and many members could not name a single improvement made by the committee. The committees were hampered by secrecy and spent too much time on trivial issues. 'PLCs' (Police Community Liaison Committees) are typically small groups of elected élites and senior RUC officers, who are neither broad-based nor anchored in the community. Important problems such as complaints against the police and major police policies never make it on to their agendas. The character of PLCs is a product of vested political interests and affinities, which operate in most communities to limit membership to non-nationalist parties, to exclude lay community members and to confine agendas to mundane matters.'[6]

One difficulty with these committees is that it is SDLP policy to boycott them on the grounds that they are powerless.

A second difficulty is that these committees are often based in the local District Councils whose contacts with local communities may be quite limited. This may be the case especially where the Council is dominated by one side or the other.

Identity issues

Most unionists, except for many in more deprived areas, identify very strongly with the RUC. They see it as the group which has done most to protect them from IRA violence and to maintain Northern Ireland as part of the UK. Many unionists have lost relatives in the RUC who were murdered by republicans. The money generated by security force jobs has been a major economic cushion for the unionist community.

One of the arguments put by nationalists is that if their Irish identity is to be recognised within Northern Ireland there will have to be changes in the identity of the police force. Secondly, nationalists and Catholics point to a long list of abuses of their identity. These charges are made much more forcefully against the B Specials, the UDR, and to a lesser extent the RIR, than against the RUC. There is hard evidence to support them.[7] There is also a wealth of anecdotal evidence. Examples are stories of B Specials and members of the UDR stopping their neighbours in rural areas and insisting on being told their names and addresses, or members of the Special Branch being able to make decisions, influenced by who was giving information, on which people would be prosecuted for traffic offences. Allegations of behaviour like this is widespread in the nationalist community, and it comes from people from very different social and political backgrounds.

An underlying source of the identity problem among a section of the nationalist community was that ultimately policing is controlled by the government, and in Northern Ireland the government is British. The implications of the Downing Street Declaration is that this will be the position as long as the majority of the people of Northern Ireland wish. But this was rejected by Sinn Féin in August 1994. It remains to be seen whether the Forum for Peace and Reconciliation will affirm the Declaration, and if so, whether Sinn Féin will then accept it.

Naming a problem such as identity is one thing. Solving it is another, and nationalists, up to the 1994 ceasefires, seldom put forward specific proposals to achieve this.

2. Options for the future

The issue of security is one that most people involved in reconciliation like to avoid, understandably enough, because there are problems with every suggestion for the future. I want to look first at the duties that Catholics have in relation to security. Then I will discuss options for changes in the Police Authority, community policing, and the advantages and disadvantages of having several police forces.

The duties of Catholics

Given the lack of accountability for the police force in Northern Ireland (a lack that is shared by other police forces in these islands), what degree of support should Catholics give to the security forces and what degree of responsibility should they take for them? The same questions can be put to Protestants.

Another way of phrasing this question is: under what conditions will and should Catholics be bound to give unambiguous support to a police service in Northern Ireland?

The first answer is that support for police in any society can never be unconditional.

Every police force in the world suffers from defects. They are in a position of power. All support for police forces must then be accompanied by critical vigilance. Power, in Acton's apt phrase, corrupts. The police themselves should be more aware of this than anyone else. They should therefore welcome any structures that act as checks and balances on them, and that thereby both control any tendency among their members to break the law, and also act as a counter to false charges against them.

The reality is that as long as the security forces and the government resist structures of greater accountability, the easier they make it for nationalists – and indeed unionists – to legitimately withhold significant support for the security forces. In strict logic, nationalists cannot be expected to take responsibility for policing if the means to do so do not exist. As long as there are no structures by which any citizen can take responsibility, nationalists, obviously, cannot do so.

This point is all the more crucial because within the nationalist community in Northern Ireland there is a great unwillingness to take responsibility for policing. Many have had negative experiences of the security forces (although it should be remembered that from 1970 to 1994 these experiences took place in the context of a cycle of violence in which some people in the nationalist community played a major role). But until nationalists are offered structures in which they will be able to exercise some responsibility for policing – and that requires structures to which the police service are accountable – they will never be forced to make concrete decisions about their duties in relation to security structures.

Nationalists often argue that policing issues can only properly be addressed in the context of an agreed political settlement. But the reverse is also true: agreement on policing is necessary as part of the process of moving towards a political settlement. Without such agreement unionist distrust is likely to remain so deep that they will block any settlement.

What we are talking about here are degrees of accountability and degrees of responsibility. The two go hand in hand: the greater the degree of accountability, the greater the duty of all citizens to take some responsibility. I do not want to suggest that because such accountability is severely limited in Northern Ireland, Catholics have no responsibility to obey the security forces. While admitting both the limits of accountability and the fact that abuses have been carried out both by individual members and by particular sections of the security forces such as MI5 or Special Branch, nonetheless Christians are duty bound to obey the security forces that currently exist in the just execution of the law unless obedience to Christ demands otherwise.[8]

What this means is threefold: a) that there is no moral basis for engaging in armed combat with members of the security forces; b) that in any particular instance the onus is on the citizen to show grounds why he or she should not obey the security forces; and c) that everyone in Northern Ireland has a moral duty to work for the development of structures in which the police – whether they are the present police force or a new one – will be properly accountable.

The legitimacy of the police force in Northern Ireland is more flawed than in many countries, because of the lack of political consensus, the unsatisfactory degree of accountability, and the abuses carried on by some members and sections of it. Nonetheless, when they act legally and justly the RUC possess a greater degree of legitimacy to police Northern Ireland than any other body that currently exists. They will continue to retain that degree of legitimacy until new structures are put in place.

But this is not an argument for the status quo in policing. Major changes are required if nationalists are to feel part of Northern Ireland. I will discuss first those changes that seem more obvious to me and then look at others which I suggest more tentatively.

MORE OBVIOUS CHANGES

Changes in the Northern Ireland Police Authority
A crucial weakness in the structure of policing in Northern Ireland is that the Police Authority has no sanctions available to it, short of dismissing the Chief Constable if the latter fails to carry out its policies. Crucially, as we have seen, it is the Chief Constable who decides what constitutes policy and what constitutes operational matters. Any police force – as with any major public body – needs operational freedom. They cannot be expected to contact the Police Authority every time they want to make an arrest. But when is an issue operational and when is it a matter of policy?

An example is Orange marches that are routed through nationalist areas. There are operational decisions to be made on these: how many personnel and armoured vehicles will be needed for the operation? Should there be army back-up? Is there likely to be violence, etc? But deciding what to do about Orange marches is also a matter of policy: it shows where the government and the police stand on respecting the identity of each tradition within Northern Ireland. So in theory the Police Authority should be able to say to the Chief Constable: 'We have taken a policy decision on this issue and have decided that in future no Orange parades shall be routed through what we deem to be nationalist areas' (provided such a decision would not be open to legal challenge). In practice the Chief Constable can reply by saying that this is an operational matter and that the RUC themselves will decide what should happen. The Police Authority should be given the power to decide when an issue is an operational one or when it is a matter of policy. (Clearly, on issues like controversial marches, the government should pass a law requiring equal treatment of different traditions).

There are other areas where the Authority could be given greater power: the right of access for all or some of its members to all operational records of the police; and the right to decide on conditions governing interrogations, including whether or not video and audio tapes of interviews of suspects should be made as a matter of policy. If the RUC argue that there are security arguments against these proposals what they are suggesting in practice is that they themselves should be trusted with security information, but members of the Police Authority should not.

Secondly, the relationship between the Secretary of State, the Police Authority, and the Chief Constable needs to be clarified in law, as the Police Authority have requested.

Thirdly, the basis of membership of the Authority should be changed. Currently the Secretary of State appoints individuals. It seems sensible to accept the Authority's suggestion that the list of bodies from which nominees are drawn should be reviewed and expanded, and that these bodies should put forward their own nominees.

If the Police Authority were given greater powers, if political parties were allowed to nominate members, and if a veto mechanism was built into the system, then what arguments would nationalists have against participating? (The veto mechanism would give a certain percentage of the Authority – say 40% – the right to veto decisions, in which case the matter would be referred up to the Secretary of State.)

An argument against changing the Police Authority on the lines suggested is that giving either side a veto might mean that very few decisions would ever be reached. However, at some stage the two communities need to work together. Because of the lack of trust and because of the need to build it, there is a need for vetoes.

In a consultation document, *Policing the community*, published in 1994, the British government admitted that the law failed to define satisfactorily the powers and responsibilities of central government, the Police Authority and the Chief Constable. They accepted that the purpose of the Police Authority should be to represent 'the community to the RUC, identify the community's priorities for policing within available resources, and hold[ing] the RUC to account for an efficient and effective delivery of these community objectives' (par 5.5). However, the document goes on to argue that any differences between the objectives of the Authority and those of the Chief Constable should be resolved by the Secretary of State. This would reduce the power of the Police Authority even further.

Secondly, the document proposed to exclude the Authority from any say in security policy or related matters. It is something of a mystery how the government are able to propose this and at the same time see the task of the Authority as identifying the community's priorities for policing. Excluding security issues from the Authority would mean taking away one of the principal powers that it should have, if the RUC are to be accountable to the community. It would mean, for example, that the Authority would probably have no say in issues such as the use of informers, the use of lethal force and plastic bullets, marches, etc.[9]

Community policing

The term 'community policing' can mean different things in the debate about the future of the security forces in Northern Ireland. For some it involves an approach to policing. For others it means the creation of new, more locally-based, police forces. In this section I want to consider it only as an approach to policing. In the following section I will look at some of the advantages and disadvantages of creating new police forces.

Community policing, understood as an approach to policing, is not social work, or community relations, although it might use some of the insights of both of these. Nor is it intelligence gathering. It is a process by which police officers working in a particular area build a series of relationships with people living and working in the area to enable them to identify problems and to work on them together. It is based on the assumption that it is impossible to police an area without the consent of those who are policed. Police can only help the members of the community in the maintenance of order. Partly because of the political situation, but partly also because of some of the policies of the RUC, there is an enormous gap between the concept of community policing and the way police work is done in Northern Ireland.

The concept of community policing is most developed in the US. It has been implemented in quite small areas and experiments have also been tried over full police departments. As part of its implementation there is extensive education for police officers: in 1993 the Kentucky State Police devoted thirty-two out of forty hours compulsory in-service training to the concept. For many officers, used to traditional policing, the training came as something of a culture shock.

Traditional methods dealt with an area of high crime by moving a large number of officers into the area and strictly enforcing the

law. The officers, who often improved their earnings because of
overtime, then moved on and crime returned to its previous levels.
The difference between this approach and that of community policing is that the officers, although they may not live in the community, are in it long enough to form relationships and to develop
approaches to crime together with local residents. When a decision
is then made to make a large number of arrests, for example of drug
dealers, it is done with the approval of the community. The community, through the police, send the drug dealers a message that
their behaviour will no longer be tolerated.[10]

The key to community policing is the relationship between the
local police and members of the community. 'The most effective
way to restore order to neighbourhoods from the community policing perspective is for the police and citizens to have a sense of ident-
ification towards one another and responsibility for the problems
facing them. Officers working in an area must have ties to it, a continuing relationship. They must know the people and the people
must know them. Without mutual trust and understanding the
restoration and maintenance of order will be elusive or perhaps
impossible to attain. Officers cannot be mercenaries, working in a
neighbourhood as strangers ... for overtime. That approach, perhaps initially effective in dealing with disorder, quickly alienates
citizens and negates any hope for long-term success.'[11]

Police-Community Liaison Committees
Despite the criticism of police-community liaison committees, these
could play a useful role within the context of wider changes in
policing. But to be effective these committees need solid roots in
housing estates. Only in this way will local people feel any ownership and be able to take some responsibility for policing. This can
only happen if such committees have realistic powers. Ensuring
that proceedings are published in the local area would help. This
would ensure that both questions raised by local people and the
answers given by the police are on record. It is one way of introducing at least a psychological element of accountability into the situation. Contacts built up between police and local people in such liaison
groups can also be useful in defusing potentially dangerous situations at a street level.

A second power such committees could be given is that their
agreement could be required for approval of the policing budget for
the local area. Failure to reach agreement would mean the issue
would be passed to a higher level, but such failure would be a public

indication of a major problem in police-community relations. That is something senior local officers would presumably be anxious to avoid.

Liaison committees should have an open agenda for policing. This would allow community groups to raise political type issues, such as the use of plastic bullets, etc., as they saw fit. There is no point at all in having local committees if they do not deal with issues that local people regard as important.

One change in recent years that should help liaison is the training courses that have been run for police members in conflict resolution. But while these courses are good they need to happen at a local level as well. It is somewhat startling that in the fourteen years I lived in Portadown, to the best of my knowledge, no Catholic priest or lay person from the town was invited to take a session with young constables, new to the town, to help them understand Catholic feelings and perceptions.

Symbols of policing

The symbols of the police in Northern Ireland are British. The name is the Royal Ulster Constabulary. The Union Jack is flown over police stations, and pictures of the British Royal family are frequently displayed. Under existing Fair Employment Legislation it is probable that such symbols would be found unlawful in other work situations because they could be construed as a discouragement to people from the nationalist community. Once again we come back to a core issue: is Northern Ireland to be British in its identity, or British-Irish? If the latter, then changes are required.

It would help to change the name to something like 'The Northern Ireland Police Service'. This gets away from the political connotations of 'Royal' and of 'Ulster'. 'Service' is a more appropriate name for the police than 'Constabulary'. It is worth noting that tensions over security may have been eased somewhat when the UDR was amalgamated into the RIR, partly because the name was changed. It is important not to overstate this case, because tensions certainly remained. But changing the name of the regiment removed a symbol that – for Nationalists – was a very negative one. The nationalist perception of the RUC is nowhere near as negative as it was of the UDR, but a name change would still help. Its advantages would not necessarily be tangible, but it could be part of a series of changes that would create a new atmosphere in relation to policing. It would help us to get to the point where nationalists would no longer feel that policing is something foreign to them and over against them.

Secondly, there is no reason to fly any flags over police stations. In a divided society like Northern Ireland, the less flags of any kind the better.

Thirdly, police personnel should keep their pictures of the Royal family in their homes, if they so desire.

MORE TENTATIVE SUGGESTIONS

The above changes in policing in Northern Ireland should be made. But on their own they are unlikely to be sufficient to persuade nationalists to accept the police to the extent of joining them. For that more radical changes are required. The difficulties in assessing these changes are twofold: they need to be workable at a practicable level, and they need to be potentially acceptable or at least tolerable to the British and Irish governments and also to the unionist community.

Changes within current police structures
New geographical based regions

A change suggested by some, including Seamus Mallon, the Justice Spokesman of the SDLP, is that the police would be divided into geographical regions.[12] The theory is that members of the police would identify with the local area and this would bond them both with each other and with the people they serve. The suggestion might work in areas where one or other community is in a strong majority. But there are likely to be continued problems where this is not the case, and where there is a history of bad relationships between the communities. A case in point is mid-Ulster: the region would include local communities with deep-seated antagonisms towards each other. But it is worth exploring the suggestion because it may work well in some areas.

Regions based on political identity

A variation of the regional proposal is that divisions should be based on political identity. Many dismiss this on the grounds that it would make political divisions deeper. But this argument needs to be investigated more closely. In 1994 over 50% of the people of Northern Ireland lived in areas with less than 10% of members of the other community. Fewer than 100,000 – approximately 7% – live in areas with an equal proportion of each religion. Of the 51 electoral wards in Belfast 16 were over 95% Protestant or Catholic. A total of 35 wards contain at least 90% of one religion.[13] This meant that there was little difficulty in deciding whether an area was nationalist or unionist. In 1986 Liam Kennedy argued the case for a re-partition of Ireland based on an analysis of District Council election returns. Re-partition is not being argued for here, but the maps in Kennedy's book show how contiguous areas of nationalists and unionists can be drawn, each containing less than 20% of the other community.[14]

Sometimes the idea of separate regions for policing based on political identity is greeted with derision in Northern Ireland. Obvious difficulties with the concept are pointed out in discussion: how could we be certain that they would not be controlled by paramilitaries? What about corruption? Would different police regions not make divisions in Northern Ireland permanent? Some of these questions are serious, and some of those who put them are genuine in their search for peace. But it is interesting to note the assumptions that are made: that it is better to make Northern Ireland as a whole a region, even though it is dominated by individuals from the unionist community than to face the problems of having more than one region; that there is no problem with the control and accountability of sections of the current police force; that collusion between loyalist paramilitaries and individual members of the security forces was a sad but inevitable reality about which little could be done; that 'we' are one community. There will be no serious progress in Northern Ireland as long as such assumptions are allowed to go unchallenged.

Assuming that the 1994 ceasefires hold, it would be quite possible to develop several police regions in Northern Ireland, some nationalist and some unionist, to patrol their respective communities. Just as electoral boundaries are changed in accordance with shifts in population so police precincts could be changed. Each region could have its own Police-Community Liaison Committee, and the different committees could be subject to the Northern Ireland-wide Police Authority.

Separate groups to deal with 'ordinary' police work?
A third proposal is that different groups would be created within the police service for different functions. So, one section might deal with intelligence work, a second with riot control, a third with paramilitary crime, etc. In fact this is the current situation, but the distinction between the different groups is often not visible to the public. The result is that the RUC as a whole gets a bad name, if, for example, Divisional Mobile Support Units, who are often called into riot situations, act over-aggressively. It would greatly help

public perceptions if there were clear differences in uniform, command structures, etc, so that people would not associate police engaged in 'ordinary' police work – which constitutes the great bulk of day-to-day police activity – with the actions of riot control or intelligence gathering agencies.

Develop Garda placements in Northern Ireland

Several people, including southern columnist Vincent Browne,[15] have suggested using the south's police force, the Garda, in a limited way in Northern Ireland. At one level what they are suggesting can be construed as a simple exchange between neighbouring police forces. A number of Gardaí would be based for limited periods in nationalist areas, and work with and under the direction of the Northern Ireland Police Service. The advantages would be that nationalists should find it easier to accept a police force which had some Gardaí working in its ranks. Further, since close relationships have been developed between the two forces it should not be too difficult to arrange such exchanges.

However, unionists inevitably would see such a move as a step towards a united Ireland. Some nationalists in deprived areas might well have as many problems with members of the Garda as with the RUC, because they object to any policing. However, the presence of Gardaí would expose this and show that their complaints had nothing to do with national identity.

More radical changes

Place policing under any new assembly

The main argument in favour of this is that if the Northern Ireland problem is to be resolved then nationalists and unionists have to work together on policing. An obvious place for them to do this is in any new assembly. Of course there would be disagreements, and vetoes would be needed, but the same would be true of any new Police Authority. Further, if a new sssembly were given control over policing the obvious candidate for ministerial control would be a nationalist. This is because it is nationalists who traditionally have had most difficulties with policing in Northern Ireland because of the identity of the state. If they were offered proper ministerial responsibility, on what grounds could they refuse it? If they accepted such responsibility, then the conflict is essentially over because there would be agreement between nationalists and unionists on the core issue.

There are of course arguments against placing policing under any new assembly. The main one is that if the aim is to build a degree of political consensus, then it is better to leave more difficult issues – and policing is certainly difficult – to a later date. Secondly, at least a section of unionists would oppose it because they are integrationists and they want any new assembly to have only minimal powers. Anything else, they believe, will strengthen the differences between Northern Ireland and Britain and thereby weaken the union.

An All-Ireland Police Authority

For northern nationalists an all-Ireland Police Authority would be very attractive because it would ensure that they would not be dominated by unionists, and it would also introduce a further buffer between the police in Northern Ireland and the British government. If there was agreement about an all-Ireland Police Authority it might make it easier for nationalists to accept the continued existence of the RUC.

The proposal would be strongly resisted by unionists on the grounds that it would give the Dublin government a decision-making role in the affairs of Northern Ireland. But such an Authority would also have a say over policing in the south. It would therefore give unionists a role in the affairs of the south reciprocal to that of the south within the north. For that reason, of course, the Dublin government is likely to resist any such proposal very strongly. But at this point nationalists, and especially Dublin governments, need to be challenged as to what they mean when they say they want to develop relationships between both parts of the island. Do they mean simply that they want a degree of power within Northern Ireland, or do they want to develop new reciprocal structures which will involve changes in the south as well?

Further, if an all-Ireland Police Authority were based on the principle of power-sharing, unionists would have the power of veto over it. If this were used it would mean matters would be referred to either the British or Irish government, depending on which had jurisdiction over the matter in question. Nationalists might conclude, because of this, that such an authority is not worthwhile, because in the end many of them want joint authority, that is a system by which the two governments control Northern Ireland together and by agreement. But that option does not seem politically possible. Both the British and the Irish governments have rejected it. In these circumstances an all-Ireland Police Authority, on which both nationalists and unionists would have a veto, might be attractive to them.

Separate police forces

Separate police forces, based on political identity, is a variation of the proposal to have such regions within one Northern Ireland police force, except that in this instance police in the regions would become separate forces. The proposal is based on the assumption that the RUC is irreformable and that we need an entirely new structure. The advantages are that one could more easily separate out the less pleasant aspects of policing, such as riot control, by putting these under the control of a Northern Ireland-wide force. Secondly, it would be much easier for nationalists to join a group that was clearly separate from the RUC. Thirdly, the proposal takes seriously the different identities that exist within Northern Ireland.

Undoubtedly, the RUC would oppose the idea of separate forces, because it would reduce their power, and in this they would be supported by the vast majority of the unionist community who identify very strongly with the RUC. Secondly, it would take a number of years to train new forces and blend them into policing as a whole in Northern Ireland. However, the Dublin government might find it easier to accept this proposal than that of an all-Ireland Police Authority, because it would not tie it into any new responsibilities.

There is nothing unusual in the proposal to have several police forces. It is the regular practice in many countries in Europe, in America, and of course, in England, Scotland and Wales. Those who argue against it need to defend themselves against the charges that they are either trying to protect the power of the RUC, or else that they are unwilling to face the consequences of taking seriously the fact that in Northern Ireland there are two identities: one British and one Irish.

Clearly, if a decision were made to set up separate police forces – and it seems to me to be a less likely option, despite its desirable elements – there would need to be unifying mechanisms between different forces. This might be achieved by each force having its own Police Authority with these in turn being subject to a Northern Ireland-wide Authority, and also to international inspection.

Other issues

Keep or disband the RUC?

The RUC are the existing police force in Northern Ireland. There are arguments for and against major changes. It would be administratively easier to keep the force as it is. There are a whole series of structures in place that any police force needs. Examples are: work practices, a community relations division, training schemes, promotion criteria, wage rates, secretarial systems, etc. Many also argue that to introduce major structural change in the RUC would be very destabilising and that this is the last thing that Northern Ireland needs as it goes through a period of deep political debate. Introducing change would 'politicise' the police. This, it is argued, would be a pity as the RUC have shown themselves to be above politics during the violence up to 1994. They can argue – not totally incredibly – that they have a degree of objectivity. In support of this it is pointed out that the RUC locked up more loyalist than republican paramilitaries and that they have withstood attacks from loyalist quarters, particularly after the signing of the Anglo-Irish Agreement. As well as this many nationalists are prepared to work with the RUC.

However, there are strong objective arguments for radical changes in policing. It is incoherent to argue that policing can be 'non-political'. There are of course many actions any police force has to take that have no connections with politics: dealing with traffic accidents, looking for missing persons, etc. But there are others that are inherently political, especially in a society with a very limited degree of consensus.

Identity

The issue of identity, as I have argued, is related to the question of how radical changes in policing need to be. The RUC are the 'Royal Ulster Constabulary'. Their identity is British, not surprisingly because most of its members would see themselves as British, and the British government controls them. Is the new Northern Ireland going to be British, or is it going to be British-Irish? If the latter, then the police force will have to be radically different.

As long as there is only one police force, it is likely to be dominated by unionists, and therefore to have a British identity. This is an important issue in local communities. In 1993, when asked what peace would mean, Gearóid Ó Caralláin, editor of the Irish language newspaper *Lá*, replied: It would mean 'British soldiers off the streets ... There would be an ordinary civilian police force. Working-class nationalists could get jobs on it. There'd be police officers in Andersonstown [in West Belfast] wearing fáinnes [the symbol used by Irish speakers] and standing under the tricolour to *Amhrán na bhFiann* [the Irish national anthem].'[16] From the standpoint of 1994 it looks as if it will be some time before we will see members of the RUC sauntering up the Falls Road in Belfast, or the main street in Crossmaglen, singing *Amhrán na bhFiann*! However, it needs to be added that strange things have happened in Northern Ireland before – notably the IRA and loyalist truces – and nothing is impossible once people decide to move out of sectarian concepts. Further, it is very difficult to tell how people will respond to the RUC if we have several years of non-violence, and the paramilitary element of police work is considerably reduced.

Having separate police forces will not however meet the need of those nationalists in Northern Ireland who want to separate policing from the British government. The police in any state are not going to be completely independent of the government. Since the majority of nationalists have accepted the principle of consent in the Downing Street Declaration, that means that the British government are going to be the ultimate authority in Northern Ireland for the foreseeable future.

Recruiting

A further issue is that of recruiting. In 1994 there were approximately 13,000 members between the RUC, the fulltime and part-time Reserves. Informed observers suggested that a force of somewhere between 5,000 and 6,500 would be needed. But less than 7% of police members are Catholics. If the force was proportional to the population the figure would be about 42%. How can a greater balance be achieved?

There is no easy answer to this question, whether it is decided to stay with one force or to create several. Clearly the number of police will be reduced if the ceasefires hold. But new members will be needed annually. Otherwise the police force will simply age and no government could afford that. What proportion of new members will be Catholics?

Fair employment legislation in Northern Ireland rules out reverse discrimination. Many nationalists would not support such discrimination in any case because it would mean that they would be offered jobs simply because they were Catholics, and not on grounds of merit. However, in the Craig-Collins Pact in 1922 it was suggested that one third of the places in the RUC would be reserved for Catholics. This never happened in practice. There are arguments for looking at some kind of similar measure, for a limited number of years, if we take seriously the need to have both nationalists and unionists involved in policing.

As with other issues, it is important not to develop fixed ideas on how a good objective, such as increasing the number of nationalists in a police force, might be attained. Changing employment patterns is seldom easy, as experience of gender discrimination shows. Some argue that less radical means might achieve the desired aim. So, the argument goes, if the ceasefires hold, part-time Reserves can be let go immediately, and full-time Reserves at a later time as their contracts run out. Since these contracts are for a maximum of three years, this would quickly bring the RUC down to about 8,500. Allowing for natural wastage it should not be too difficult to bring this figure down to the estimated required level of about 5,000-6,500. New recruits would also have to be brought in during this period to avoid having an ageing force. If 50% of the recruits were from the nationalist community, then after approximately ten years one could expect about 25% of the police to be nationalist.

There are all sorts of assumptions in this argument, chief among them that 50% of new recruits would be nationalists. Given the antipathy of many nationalists to joining the present police this is extremely optimistic. However, the argument for changing the balance of the police through less radical means should at least be addressed.

Conclusion

It may be possible to reorganise the RUC in such a way that nationalists will be attracted to joining it, and that the principles governing policing laid down by the UN might be met. If this were the case it would certainly be easier for such proposals to gain political acceptance, given the political influence of the RUC. But the difficulties in making the force truly representative of, and accountable and responsive to, both communities remain considerable.

Which combination of the above options is best? There can be no hard and fast answer to this question. It is a question of balance, and one person's dream will be another's nightmare. My own tentative answer is that I would be open to some of the following combinations. Each combination would contain the following elements:

  – A Northern Ireland Police Authority with greatly increased powers, with organisations nominating their own members to it, with a weighted majority required for certain policy decisions connected with identity issues, and with realistic sanctions it can employ if the police fail to carry out its policies;

  – Policing to be done on the basis of community policing;

  – Clearly separate structures – if there is to be one police service – to deal with difficult policing issues, such as security, riot control, etc;

- A properly independent complaints procedure;
- Developing new Police Liaison Committees with strong input from local community groups;
- Changes in the name and other symbols of the police.

On their own, these changes would be insufficient. But if any of the following options were added to them, the balance might be correct:

a) An all-Ireland Police Authority;

b) Within one Northern Ireland-wide police service:

- Separate geographical regions, which also take account of different political identities;
- Exchanges with the Garda leading to a considerable number of Gardaí operating under the control of the Northern Ireland police within nationalist areas;

c) Separate police services linked to one Northern Ireland Police Authority, with federal-wide forces to deal with issues such as intelligence gathering, riot control, etc.

Whatever combination is chosen it needs to take account of two realities:

a) The principle of consent in the Downing Street Declaration which means that ultimately the British government will be making the laws that govern policing in Northern Ireland, as long as the majority of its people so wish;

b) That the people of Northern Ireland are not all British in their cultural and national identity. Very nearly 50% of them are Irish. The state and the political structures controlling it, including the framework of policing, need to take account of this.

As I have maintained throughout this chapter, suggestions in the area of policing need to be tentative, because it is a notoriously difficult subject in a divided society. It is an issue that needs to be debated widely. I therefore support the call of the Committee for the Administration of Justice for an international commission to be set up to look into this issue. This is a particularly useful suggestion because we can learn something from what has worked, and what has not worked, in other societies.

This is also an issue in which churches, if they were inspired by the gospel message of reconciliation, forgiveness, community and conflict, could play a very useful role. This would be by challenging their own members about the duties which they have in this area as members of society. Further, given the numbers that attend churches in Northern Ireland, prayerful and communal reflection which emphasised the sacrifices all sides need to make, could be a powerful mechanism in developing the generosity that is needed to solve this issue. It could also help all of us to become more aware of the prejudices we all have, and thereby make us a little more humble in putting forward proposals. I hope I have not offended against these principles myself.

Notes:

1 Adopted by General Assembly on 17th December, resolution 34/169 of 1979.

2 *cf* David B. Rottman and Philip F. Tormey, 'Respectable Crime: occupational and professional crime in the Republic of Ireland', *Studies*, Vol 75, No 1.

3 Brian Nelson acted as a government agent from 1983, while he was an intelligence officer in the UDA, one of the main loyalist paramilitary groups. He was arrested in 1992.

4 The Police Authority for Northern Ireland, *The Work of the Police Authority, 1991-1994*, Belfast 1994.

5 Paper submitted by Police Authority of Northern Ireland to the Northern Ireland Office, November 1993, in response to the inquiry conducted by Sir Patrick Sheehy on policing.

6 Ronald Weitzer, 'Northern Ireland Police Liaison Committees' in *Policing and Society*, Vol 2, 1992, pp 233-243.

7 *cf* Committee on the Administration of Justice, forthcoming book on harassment.

8 *Breaking Down the Enmity*, Belfast 1993, p 186.

9 *cf* The Committee on the Administration of Justice, *Policing the community: A response by the CAJ*, Belfast, 1994.

10 *cf* Walter Tangel, 'Community oriented policing: a Jefferson County, Kentucky experience', National Lodge, *Fraternal Order of Police Journal*, Fall/Winter 1993, pp 46-52.

11 ibid, p 52.

12 *The Irish Times*, 7 November 1994.

13 Source: David McKittrick, Ireland Correspondent, *The Independent*.

14 *Two Ulsters: A case for re-partition*, Belfast 1986. *cf* page 57 for four maps showing different options for Northern Ireland regions, each with a greater or lesser minority.

15 *cf The Irish Times*, 2 November 1994.

16 Suzanne Breen 'Peace would bring Northern Ireland up off its knees', *The Irish Times*, 18 December 1993.

Conclusion

In the 1970s and 1980s a tremendous emphasis was placed on liberation theology. This started in the context of the oppression of the poor in Central America. Essentially, liberation theology is a method in which a particular situation is first analysed politically, socially and economically and then subjected to a faith critique in which great emphasis is placed on scripture. In this process no attempt is made to be impartial: priority is given to the rights of the poor, who are defined as 'the people'. Further it is accepted that analysis cannot be done except in the context of a commitment to those who are deprived. This must involve conflict with vested interests.

The method of liberation theology has influenced this book. However, the theme of reconciliation has also been emphasised. For some there is a conflict between these themes on the grounds that reconciliation is a soft approach which avoids conflict and in the end maintains the status quo. That means that the poor stay poor.

Reconciliation in practice can often be like this. Much ecumenical work in Northern Ireland, for example, avoids criticism of the security forces because only in this way will many unionists stay involved. This illustrates a central element in the Northern Ireland conflict that is different from the Latin American context: in Northern Ireland the constitutional issue dominates everything so that class issues cannot be properly addressed. Thus in Catholic areas of Portadown over 70% of the population are unemployed. In some Protestant areas of the town the figure is over 50%. But what dominates the minds of most people is not unemployment, or how people can work together to overcome it, but the political situation and the violence caused by it. Duncan Morrow has remarked aptly: 'All attempts to set up specifically class-based parties have foundered in the past on the national question.'[1]

For communities under threat – and both communities in Northern Ireland are under threat – nothing matters as much as survival. Further, the source of the threat is always defined as the other community and this applies to rich and poor within that community.

This is in part the reason why a theology of reconciliation, which must also be just, is essential as well as making use of the method and assumptions of a theology of liberation. To define the poor or deprived in Northern Ireland is not possible without including both nationalist and unionist poor.

The reality is that we will all remain victims to a degree in Northern Ireland until a theology of reconciliation, as well as one of liberation, becomes much more central in social, political and ecclesiastical life. This is true for those, like many republicans, who saw, and in some cases continue to see, themselves as second-class citizens. It is true for unionist working-class people who for many years have been convinced that nationalists were making social, political, and economic gains at their expense. It is true for Catholics who, in religious terms, do not appreciate the fears that Protestants have of their church or the possibilities that they have of a richer experience of Christ by learning about the good things in Protestant Churches. It is true for those Protestants who need to come to terms with their fears of the Catholic Church and also to get to know that church much more fully as it really is, warts and all. It is true for members of the security forces who need to come to terms with both the nationalist and the unionist working-class communities. It is true for British people who need to recognise the harm that has been done in the past to Northern Ireland people, both nationalist and unionist. It is true for the people of the Republic of Ireland who need to face the apathy and ambivalence which many have had for so long towards the north. Finally, it is true for those bereaved by the conflict as they struggle to come to terms with their loss.

I have argued that reconciliation as well as justice is at the centre of the Christian story, and that in that story one is not possible without the other. Forgiveness is part of reconciliation but only part of it. It is the task of the victim to offer it. But there is no reconciliation until those who cause the suffering come to terms with what they have done and seek the forgiveness of those they have harmed. Until they do that they remain outside God's community and are the object of her anger.

A theology of reconciliation can easily be misused to overlook or neglect the rights of those who are economically deprived. It remains true that, whatever the outcome of the political struggle in Northern Ireland, most of those on the bottom of the economic pile, in common with their brothers and sisters in other countries, are likely to remain there. This is not to say that their plight is hopeless, or that they are powerless. President Robinson has made visible in the Republic the work of many deprived groups, often made up mostly of women. While they may seldom succeed in attaining the material benefits of the middle classes – and they are as entitled to those benefits as anyone else – nonetheless they can discover values and self-worth both in themselves and in their community that can enrich their lives.

However, encouraging deprived people to grow in personal self-confidence is nowhere near sufficient as an aim for the Christian community. People who are deprived economically need and deserve greater political power than they can have in a conventional democracy. It may be that in facing up to the political requirements to serve a divided community within Northern Ireland we may eventually come to an equally important question: how can we devise structures that give a disproportionate power to the minority who are economically deprived so that their needs may gain a more important place on the national agenda? All the poverty programmes in the world are no replacement for giving deprived people a say in political power, so that they are part of the process of agenda-setting.

It might be argued that deprived people already have this through being able to start pressure groups. But they are not competing on a level playing field. The forces that control society in any modern democracy are the middle classes. With all the analysis and work that was done on poverty in the Republic and in the north throughout the 1970s and 1980s, there were more deprived people at the start of the 1990s than twenty years earlier. Well meaning statements had been made, but the decisions had been taken by those in power, and the end result was greater poverty.

If there is going to be a change in poverty in Ireland more radical steps need to be taken. One possibility is that certain areas of the country, because they have a great degree of poverty, should be given seats as of right in the Dáil or in any new power-sharing executive within Northern Ireland.

It is interesting to note that the reaction of many people to a suggestion like this is to dismiss it as naïve and unworkable. But the same people have no problem accepting the concept of power-sharing within Northern Ireland. Yet what is the difference between giving disproportionate political power to people because they are deprived and doing so because they are a political minority?

Many of the same problems apply: would the deprived or the nationalists have a veto? If so, over what areas of government? What would happen if there were a stalemate? How would deprived or nationalist areas be defined? What mechanisms would there be for changing constituency boundaries as the population got less deprived or less nationalist?

Of course power sharing is nowhere near a complete answer to issues of poverty or sectarian divisions. What it might do, though, is give greater power to groups that are currently marginalised from political processes. That might well lead to greater attention and urgency being given to the problems they face, which would mean these issues would be given greater priority. Part of the reason why poverty is so prevalent now is that, in the end, issues of poverty always take second place to issues of wealth. (For example governments often concentrate on economic growth which very often leads to wealth for a few and continued unemployment for many.) Changing the balance of power in the Dáil and in any new executive in the north might make it more difficult for the rich to get away with scandals such as those investigated by the Beef Tribunal which reported in 1994.

The challenge facing us with regard to sectarian divisions within Northern Ireland is to come up with proposals for political structures that take account of the actual identities of the groups living within the north and their relationships with both the Republic and with Britain. The task, as we have suggested in this book, is not impossible and we are hopefully in the last phase of the conflict. Any structures we come up with could become models for other countries in how to handle social, political and religious divisions.

Good states do not get built by accident. They come into existence because of hard political thinking and action. They depend on a vision. That vision has to take account of the needs both of individuals and groups within the body politic. It also has to deal with external relationships. The vision has to be inclusive. It has to balance power between different groups and classes. It has to protect minorities. To some extent it has to be a dream to which all can relate. It has to be a means by which one can have pride in the state and identify with its people.

We do not have such a state on the island of Ireland, north or south. Nor does the UK. We have political entities in which economic injustice is structured. We have a UK State in which the 'greatness' of Britain is still tied into militarism, which is partly why the UK was involved in two major military arenas within a decade: the Falklands/Malvinas (1982) and the Gulf (1991). The commitment of the UK government to violence is at least as great as that of any paramilitary group and, for the most part, no less immoral.

In the Republic we have a country that still depends to a degree on the myth of unity. Its national anthem glorifies armed conflict. It has failed to deal seriously to date with the issue of poverty. However, the Republic may be coming to terms with the existence of Northern Ireland. It can play a crucial role in helping northerners, both nationalist and unionist, to come to terms with each other.

The issue facing us all in Ireland and Britain is to imagine our future differently from the way our ancestors imagined theirs. This book has looked at what that might mean for nationalists and Catholics. The changes suggested need to be mirrored by equally costly changes in the British/unionist/Protestant community. The motivation for such changes lies in the Christian scriptures and especially in the life of Christ. These suggest criteria for changes: they must be inclusive, they must take account of the situation of deprived people, they must incorporate forgiveness and compassion, as well as a determination to confront oppression.

One of the few things that unites all political parties in the north is the need for a Bill of Rights or constitution. We need 'Founding Fathers and Mothers' who can take on the task of drafting such a document.

The burden of the argument presented in this book is that the only way in which the different groups on this island can have a fruitful, human existence is through a greater degree of justice and reconciliation. Politically I have tried to show that this is true in the north. So much suffering has been caused mainly because the two groups were not able to give each other sufficient space and recognition.

The ceasefires announced by the IRA on 31 August and by the Combined Loyalist Military Command on 13 October 1994 were the most hopeful events that have taken place perhaps since 1968. It meant that the main protagonists of violence were now committed to politics. That set an entirely new context within which difficult questions could be addressed. The IRA ceasefire was also a sign of quite extraordinary change in an organisation. While loyalists had increased their violence and effectiveness in killing since about 1990, the IRA had certainly not been defeated militarily by 1994. Nor had they achieved their aims, especially of persuading the British government to announce their intention to withdraw from Northern Ireland, or to commit themselves to persuading the unionists of the merits of a united Ireland.

That ceasefire was therefore an example of a group perhaps seeing the dead-end involved in violence and also the possibilities open to them through politics. The change in the attitude of Sinn Féin was helped by dialogues in which they had been engaged over several years with small groups of Protestants. This was an example of costly reconciliation and justice at work because it was no easy matter for these Protestants to face into dialogue with people who supported the killing of members of the unionist community. Nor was it easy for Sinn Féin members, given the feelings they had about oppression and their view that Protestant Churches were not particularly interested in justice.

In the course of this book I have tried to show that just as political realities show the need for reconciliation and justice and that these can only go together, so Christian theology shows the same thing. Our God is a God of community. We cannot share in the life of this God unless we also live as part of God's community in this world. This was true for the people of the Hebrew scriptures who separated themselves from the people of God's covenant when they acted unjustly towards the poor. It was true in the life of Jesus and in his preaching and living of peace, forgiveness, reconciliation, conflict, suffering and hope. All his parables, his teaching and the way he lived show that we can have no part in his life unless we love tenderly and act justly.

Perhaps part of our problem in Ireland, north and south, is that, although at a certain level we are a very religious people, we do not have the question that so concerned the Jewish people: how could they know that they were accepted by God? The answer the Pharisees gave was by keeping the law. It was the wrong answer, as Jesus pointed out. The right answer was compassion. But in our own situation we seem to assume that we are all right with God, as long as we keep out of major sin.

The story of the scriptures and the teaching of Christian theology tell us that God will never abandon us, that from God's side faithfulness will be eternal. But they also tell us that unless we are in just and reconciling relationships with those with whom we share this world, we will not be able to recognise God. That teaching will be true for all of us when our time comes to meet God face to face.

It is also true for us today as we move through the world which we have been lent for a few short years.

Notes:
1 Duncan Morrow, Derek Birrell, John Greer and Terry O'Keefe, *The Churches and inter-community relations*, Coleraine: The Centre for the Study of Conflict, University of Ulster, 1991.

Index